Ruwaida Amer

Stories from the war on Gaza

We do not wish to be more heroic, nor do we wish
to be greater victims. We want simply to be ordinary mortals ...
— Mahmoud Darwish

A Palaver Book. Copyright © 2025. Ruwaida Amer author.
All rights reserved. No part of this book may be reproduced, stored in a retrieval system or transmitted by any means, electronic, mechanical, photocopying, recording, or otherwise, without written permission from the publisher, author, or illustrator except in the case of brief quotations embodied in critical articles or reviews.
Typeface: Tiempos [Klim, NZ] Design & typesetting: Ian Robertson
ISBN: 978-0-6455881-7-0
For additional information, bulk or educational purchases, and other resources, please contact Ethica Projects Pty Ltd.
c/o Paul Komesaroff: paul.komesaroff@monash.edu
First Palaver edition published September 2025.

www.palaver.com
Palaver is an imprint of Ethica Projects Pty. Ltd.
10 Barnato Grove Armadale Victoria 3143 Australia

Ruwaida Amer

Stories from the war on Gaza

EDITORS
PAUL KOMESAROFF & SALLY GARDNER

PALAVER

Contents

7
Introduction: Paul Komesaroff & Sally Gardner

9
Preface: After a year of war in Gaza we ask every day if it will be our last
9 OCTOBER 2024

15
Does Israel want to exterminate Gaza's children?
13 NOVEMBER 2023

19
Israel's war on Gaza silences its historic mosques
1 JANUARY 2024

23
How Israel killed a disabled man
2 JANUARY 2024

25
War on Gaza: Displaced Palestinians find no shelter in Rafah
16 JANUARY 2024

29
The olive tree, symbol of Palestine and mute victim of Israel's war on Gaza
22 JANUARY 2024

33
Infections increase in Gaza
9 MAY 2024

35
Motherhood during genocide
23 MAY 2024

39
Hunger is rapidly getting worse in Gaza
17 JUNE 2024

41
When Israel attacked hungry children
19 JULY 2024

43
Netzarim corridor: Israel's "axis of death" for Palestinians
24 DECEMBER 2024

49
"Broken": Domestic violence impacts women and children in Gaza
25 DECEMBER 2024

55
I cannot believe our nightmare is over in Gaza
18 JANUARY 2025

59
Beatings, diseases, humiliation: A Palestinian doctor's year in Israeli jails
18 FEBRUARY 2025

65
By imposing a maze of checkpoints, Israel is replicating West Bank conditions in Gaza
26 FEBRUARY 2025

69
"We want to live": Rage at Israel fuses with ire at Hamas as protests rock Gaza
27 MARCH 2025

73
"I am not a number, I am a real story from Gaza. Remember it."
6 APRIL 2025

77
"Rafah became my home after displacement. It is now being erased."
12 APRIL 2025

81
A ruined university in northern Gaza becomes a refuge.
15 APRIL 2025

85
In Gaza the Nakba is being relived in 2025
15 MAY 2025

89
Gaza's Al-Baqa Cafe was a sanctuary amid the genocide. Now it lies in ruins.
3 JULY 2025

95
"We live in a state of chaos"
10 JULY 2025

99
"We are starving"
21 JULY 2025

105
Acknowledgments

Ruwaida Amer at work,
interviewing displaced Palestinians.
(Image courtesy the author.)

INTRODUCTION
Paul Komesaroff & Sally Gardner

> **Ruwaida Amer shows us from the inside what it is that we are seeing on our television screens and news feeds. She challenges the cool insouciance the world has developed towards the endless destruction ... the relentless, systematic cruelty of the Israeli bombardments.**

Ruwaida Amer's stories of daily life in Gaza over the two years following October 7, 2023 are at once deeply disturbing and intensely inspiring.

The young Palestinian teacher and freelance journalist bears witness to almost unimaginable atrocity. She shows us what it is like to be confronted on a daily basis with the spectacle of death and destruction, in streets, homes, schools, hospitals and places of worship, with the visible, desperate suffering of ordinary citizens, including children, in their tens or hundreds of thousands. She records the pain of ordinary people caught up in a brutal, destructive conflict where no-one is spared. She describes in careful detail the personal impact of the relentless, systematic cruelty of the Israeli bombardments. She shows us what it means for grief and loss to become a daily, commonplace occurrence. She exposes the tearing apart of relationships and ways of life that had provided fragile sustenance over decades of assault. She tells us what it feels like to experience starvation.

Ruwaida shows us from the inside what it is that we are seeing on our television screens and news feeds. She challenges the cool insouciance the world has developed towards the endless destruction of buildings, the pathetic cries of the victims as they scrape desperately through the rubble looking for lost loved ones, the frantic and hopeless dashes to hospitals, themselves targets of missiles and artillery bombardments. The simplicity and clarity of her prose cuts through the sanitised bureaucratic language of governments and the media, annulling the banal, insincere expressions of disapprobation.

But out of the cacophony of war and bland chatter her voice sounds a pure and clear message of hope. Against the force of overwhelming military might a young woman bears witness to the ongoing possibility of care, commitment, loyalty and love.

... /

Against the ugly machines of destruction she gives graceful testimony that truth is still possible, however fragile and indistinct it may appear. Her voice provides an affirmation that even in the midst of atrocity all is not completely lost.

Because of Ruwaida — and her fellow witnesses — the cries of the dead children of Gaza will never be completely silenced. Because of her, their memories will never be fully erased. This is a small spark of hope, barely discernible amid the blinding flashes of destructive force, but it is a spark nonetheless.

-

PREFACE
After a year of war in Gaza we ask every day if it will be our last

9 October 2024

SOURCE: abc NEWS INTERNATIONAL

> At the start of the war the bombing was very violent and seemed so random; we all felt that we could be targeted at any time, in any place. Every night we would go to bed terrified that the bombs would fall on us or at least near us.

GAZA STRIP — A year ago, my life was very different. I had a routine. I would wake up in the morning to go to work. I was a teacher and a freelance journalist. I loved my students and writing stories. I would move between the cities in Gaza without barriers or fear. Everything was available, I could buy what I needed. Gaza was wonderful and full of beauty. All along the coast were fun places and I would meet friends, and we would enjoy ourselves. I was happy with my life. But then everything changed.

When we woke up on October 7, 2023, to the sounds of missiles, we did not understand what was happening. And initially I thought it would be a short war, but it just keeps on going. I can hardly believe we have been living like this for a year.

Our lives are so hard now. We struggle to get water and food; electricity and internet access are both scarce. Death and destruction are everywhere. I have lost count of the amount of people I know who have died.

There have been times when all communication with the rest of the world was cut off. Both the internet and phone lines went down and Gaza was completely isolated. I remember we were living in abject terror, fearing that we would die and no one would know anything about it. We have become used to war now, and some people in Gaza are so tired of it they say they would even welcome death.

I remember at the start of the war the bombing was very violent and seemed so random; we all felt that we could be targeted at any time, in any place. Every night we would go to bed terrified that the bombs would fall on us or at least near us. There came a time for me and my family that the fear was so great, and the bombing so heavy, that we moved to a nearby hospital, the European Hospital near Khan Yunis, for shelter.

... /

> **I started receiving the tragic news that some of my students had been killed ... I cried over the loss of my colleagues as well ... The news of people I knew and loved dying just kept on coming.**

It was a difficult, cold night at the end of October 2023. We were especially afraid for my mother who is 55 years old and suffers from spinal cord disease. She walks very slowly and felt that she would not be able to save herself or help us escape if there was heavy bombing around our house. So, we went to the hospital in the hope that we might be safer there. We spent the night huddled together outside in the parking lot surrounded by other families shivering.

We looked at the sky and heard the sounds of warplanes and explosions and waited for dawn to come. We felt humiliated, and scared even in the hospital, so we decided from then on we would stay at home. The memory of that night, listening to the explosions and seeing the sky light up with bombs, will stay with me forever. But we didn't realise then that our suffering was just beginning.

I started receiving the tragic news that some of my students had been killed. Issa, Habeeba and Salma. They were wonderful students, I loved them very much. I cried over the loss of my colleagues as well. I could not believe the news of their deaths. It all felt like I was in some kind of never-ending nightmare. The news of people I knew and loved dying just kept on coming.

After a year of this, it's nearly impossible to find any joy in life. We have lost our hope. We have no desire to go on, we have lost our passion. As a journalist, I personally struggle when I write stories about people and hear their stories of grief and suffering. Despair and loss is everywhere in Gaza, visible in everyone's eyes.

Toward the start of the conflict we had a brief moment of hope. On November 24, a week-long cease-fire began. There were celebrations in the streets. We had a respite from the bombs. At that time, I felt safe. I moved around freely. I did not hear the sounds of planes. It was like we could go back to our old life.

But it didn't last, and things were about to get much worse for my family. When the cease-fire agreement ended we woke up to the sound of heavy shelling in the city of Khan Yunis. The war was coming closer to us.

My home is to the east of Khan Yunis, located between that southern city and Rafah. At the beginning of December, the Israeli army began its ground operation in Khan Yunis. The soldiers had

> **Once the Israeli army had left the area, my sister returned and was devastated by the damage she saw. Much of Gaza has become a wasteland and my sister's home was no exception. It was largely ruined.**

advanced into the city and closed Salah al-Din Street which leads from my area to the city centre. This also meant we were cut off from my sister who lives on the other side of the city, to the west. My sister has two children, and we were constantly worrying about them. We were afraid that we would lose one, or both, of them. The only way out for us to get to my sister then was to go via Rafah because the army had not yet attacked there.

Then the Israel Defence Forces suddenly attacked the west of the city and my sister was forced to evacuate. She managed to flee to safety in time and moved in with us. While she was with us, she was in a constant state of fear and anxiety about her home. Her children were always asking about their home, and when they could go back home. After three months, in March, we learned that her home had been severely damaged. She had essentially lost it.

Once the Israeli army had left the area, my sister returned and was devastated by the damage she saw. Much of Gaza has become a wasteland and my sister's home was no exception. It was largely ruined.

My 3-year-old nephew Adam and his 5-year-old sister Rital were heartbroken when they saw their home. They asked where their room had gone, where were their toys? Why had this happened? Adam has an imaginary friend called Spider-Man and he told me that Spider-Man had offered to help rebuild the house.

Rital and Adam hate their home now. The apartment has been burned in parts; smoke stains scar the wall. It has no doors or windows; the walls are mostly destroyed and they can see the street from it. We have tried to fix it, but it is still very cold at night and we are worried about winter coming.

Rital can remember life before the war and always says how much she misses it — going to restaurants, going shopping and buying new clothes with her mother. But Adam can't seem to remember life before the war. When he sees pictures of Rital's memories, he asks about them in great detail, wishing he had been a part of this seemingly beautiful life.

The children are seriously distressed by the war. They hate the sound of the planes and the bombing and they often flinch in fear.

.../

> **The children are seriously distressed by the war. They hate the sound of the planes and the bombing and they often flinch in fear. They know that their kindergarten was completely destroyed. They have become too used to death and destruction and are now old beyond their years, frighteningly so.**

They know that their kindergarten was completely destroyed. They have become too used to death and destruction and are now old beyond their years, frighteningly so. They have a whole new vocabulary related to war, displacement and destruction.

And just when we thought things couldn't get any worse for my family, they did. At the beginning of July 2024, the army issued evacuation orders for different areas in Khan Yunis, including my residential area. The war was now, literally, on our doorstep.

I felt that my heart would stop from the sadness, because I had seen what had happened in the other evacuated areas — utter destruction. People returned and did not find their homes. I was begging my family not to leave our house.

We had hoped that maybe as we were near the European Hospital the area might be safe, and that the hospital would continue to operate normally and not evacuate its staff. But the Israeli military advanced, and the hospital, like many other hospitals in Gaza, was evacuated.

The entire neighbourhood was cleared out. My family felt they had no choice but to leave too. We had no other place to go except my sister's destroyed home. We couldn't go to the tent cities. My mother would not have survived.

We gathered our belongings in a truck and left, alongside thousands of other people doing the same. It was a very painful scene. The road was crowded and very difficult to navigate as much of it had been destroyed. We had lost all the landmarks of our city. They were reduced to unrecognisable rubble.

We entered the neighbourhood where my sister lives and saw such great destruction; it was as if a devastating natural disaster had hit the place. Our faces were tired and sad, scarred by what we had seen along the way. We started moving our things to my sister's apartment on the fourth floor.

When I first got there, I was shocked by the scene. What was this destroyed place? We tried to fix it as best we could, make it more inhabitable by putting up tarpaulin and nylon for some protection from the elements. We stayed for two weeks and they passed with great difficulty, every moment I felt my heart was burning as if I had left my soul at home. I saw one family on my sister's street

> I fear the sound of missiles. I wait for them to fall and explode to know if they are close to me or not. They say that those who die do not feel or hear the missile, so I try to remind myself that hearing it is a good sign.

had pitched a tent in their bombed-out home, they were so desperate to be "home."

I fear the sound of missiles. I wait for them to fall and explode to know if they are close to me or not. They say that those who die do not feel or hear the missile, so I try to remind myself that hearing it is a good sign. That was until I had a very close call.

On August 16, I was in my house on the second floor. It was late and I hadn't told my family I wasn't in bed. My father was sleeping in an open area on the roof because the weather was very hot. I heard the sound of a missile falling. I turned off my phone and I sat on the floor waiting for it to explode. When it exploded, the whole house shook. Bricks, shrapnel and glass fell everywhere. I screamed and screamed for someone to come and save me. I felt too afraid to go down to the lower floor, terrified that something might have happened to my family down there. My mother and sister were in the lower floor, while my brother was in the street with his friends.

I went downstairs but could not see anything as the smoke and dust in the air was so thick. My entire body was hurting. Thankfully none of my family died in the incident. Miraculously my father who had been on the roof was ok. But since then, I have been suffering from severe backache.

And, while we survived that incident, who knows if we will be lucky another time.

This war has extinguished the life inside of me. I had many dreams — one was to establish a learning centre for scientific innovation in Gaza; another was to travel. A girl in her thirties has many dreams, a passion for work, and positive energy. But now I am just waiting for this war to end and asking every day will I survive it or not. And beyond that we all ask — what does Gaza's future look like? How will we rebuild our lives? Are we meant to just get used to this kind of destruction?

•

https://abcnews.go.com/International/reporter-life-in-gaza-after-year-of-war-israel-hamas/story?id=114559398

Does Israel want to exterminate Gaza's children?

13 November 2023
SOURCE: THE ELECTRONIC INTIFADA

The number of children confirmed to have been killed is now approaching 5000 ... but the real figure for child deaths is far higher.

Gaza's children are living through a horror movie during the day and a nightmare after dark. Gaza's children did not choose this situation. It was imposed on them by Israel. Gaza's children did not choose death.

They have big dreams that they think about every day. They believe that their parents are superheroes who can make those dreams come true. Their parents have told the children that dreams can be realised when they grow up. But the reality — a reality imposed by Israel — is that so many children in Gaza do not grow up. They are killed before they can grow up.

The children of Gaza are experiencing the worst days of their lives. They know that Israeli warplanes are targeting them. It is by no means the first time that children have been targeted. Children comprised a large proportion of Gaza's martyrs during a major Israeli attack in May 2021.

But the intensity of the current war is unprecedented.

The number of children confirmed to have been killed is now approaching 5,000. As Gaza's hospitals are being attacked and forced to close and the health ministry is unable to update casualty data — and huge numbers are trapped under rubble — the real figure for child deaths is far higher.

Terror every day ... Some of those killed were newborn babies. Is killing childhood in Gaza really the goal of Israel's war?

Israel is displaying its inhumanity by robbing children of their right to live in peace. Children fear the sound of missiles and explosions. They are exhausted because they are deprived of sleep and rest. They have to move with their parents from one place to another. They hope to find safety. But there is none.

... /

> **Many children have written their names on their hands and feet. They have done so to ensure that if they die, they will not die anonymously. They will not be numbers.**

Sarah al-Saadi is aged 14. "This is not a war," she said. "This is the extermination of children. How can the world look at the scenes of children under the rubble as if it is something normal? No one feels for us ... I have not heard anyone saying, 'Stop the war for the sake of Gaza.' We live in terror every day. We are afraid of the sounds of missiles and the sounds of tank shells. They never stop."

Sarah and her family have taken shelter in a school run by the UN agency for Palestine refugees (UNRWA). They went there, she said, "to escape death ... We walked for a long distance under bombardment. They [the Israelis] showed no mercy or pity to the children."

Sarah has talked to other children at the UNRWA school about her experiences. "We all need to speak and be heard," she said. "This is a very scary world. We are children. And like the other children of the world, we have the right to learn, the right to play and the right to live in peace."

Is death approaching?

Many children have written their names on their hands and feet. They have done so to ensure that if they die, they will not die anonymously. They will not be numbers. Many children cried before writing their names. They felt that death was approaching them.

"I saw many videos of children who were torn to pieces," said Reem Salama, 10. "Nobody knew who they were. I saw pictures of children writing their names on their hands. That's why I sat in the schoolyard and wrote my name on my hands and feet. Other children came around and I wrote their names for them. I felt sad but this is life in Gaza."

"Instead of learning, playing, watching TV, spending time at home, we are writing our names on our bodies," she added. "We are afraid that we will die without anyone knowing about us."

Adults are struggling to offer children comfort as Israel's bombardment continues. Khaleda Zakaria, 45, said, "This is a war against children. I cried so hard when I saw children writing their names on their hands and feet. Some of them asked me, 'Does this mean we are going to die?' I told them, 'No, this is just a game.'"

> "I miss my grandfather and my grandmother and other relatives … I miss my home. We had to leave it because of the bombing. I am tired of sleeping in classrooms and searching for water … I am tired of the sound of missiles."

Zakaria notes that problems associated with trauma, such as bed-wetting at night and trembling during the day, are widespread. "The sounds of missiles frighten them a lot," she said. "They experience fear and anxiety all the time. If a missile falls next to us, they cannot sleep at all during the night out of fear that someone will target them. I have five children and they are all living through the same terrible experience. I just wish the war would end and I often pray for that."

Children who are unable to attend classes and routines that give their lives some stability have collapsed.

"I used to complain about how I had to wake up early for school," said Ahmad Abu al-Rous, 13. "I couldn't wait until the weekend or until we had vacations. Now, I hope that school will start again. I miss my friends."

"I miss my grandfather and my grandmother and other relatives," he said. "I miss my home. We had to leave it because of the bombing. I am tired of sleeping in classrooms and searching for water for my family. I am tired of the sound of missiles. I am tired of everywhere being crowded. I hope the war stops. I hope that the world hears our voices."

•

https://electronicintifada.net/content/does-israel-want-exterminate-gazas-children/40616

Israel's war on Gaza silences its historic mosques

1 January 2024
SOURCE: MIDDLE EAST EYE (MEE)

> "We no longer hear the call to prayer in our neighbourhood due to the complete destruction of the eastern area in the city, including the mosques."

In a series of targeted strikes during its ongoing bombardment of Gaza, the Israeli army laid waste to dozens of mosques, including the iconic Al-Omari Mosque, renowned for its historical and archaeological significance. The destruction has left Palestinians, both in Gaza and in the diaspora, mourning the loss of a mosque with a unique heritage.

Since 7 October, Israeli forces have completely or partially destroyed more than 300 mosques and three churches. As a consequence, the affected neighbourhoods now suffer a void during prayer times, missing the soul-stirring call to prayer that once echoed throughout the city.

"We no longer hear the call to prayer in our neighbourhood due to to the complete destruction of the eastern area in the city, including the mosques," said Khaled Abu Jame, a 25-year-old resident of the southern city of Khan Yunis. "Residents here now follow the call to prayer through their phones. This war has been unlike anything we've experienced before. Mosques, a symbol of our faith, have been targeted indiscriminately."

Reflecting on the cherished memories associated with the Al-Omari Mosque, Jame emphasised its central role in daily life. "We have beautiful memories of the mosque. We used to pray there daily, perform Ramadan and Eid prayers, read the Quran, and meet as friends," he told MEE.

Heart of community

Jame pointed out that mosques have been deeply woven into their lives since childhood. The call to prayer serves as their morning wake-up and the mosque stands as a guiding landmark for anyone searching for their homes, he explained. It's more than a mere building; it represents "the heart of the community".

... /

> **Jame emphasised that rebuilding their neighbourhood is closely tied to reconstructing the mosques since these places are not a secondary consideration but rather the primary foundation of their lives.**

Jame emphasised that rebuilding their neighbourhood is closely tied to reconstructing the mosques since these places are not a secondary consideration but rather the primary foundation of their lives.

The Grand Omari Mosque was established during Caliph Omar bin al-Khattab's reign. Once a Roman temple and later a church, it became the largest mosque post-Islamic conquest. Located in Gaza's old city, near Palestine Square, it spans 4,100 sqm, with a courtyard of 1,190 sqm accommodating over 3,000 worshippers.

"I never thought this war would destroy mosques," Gaza native Saeed Labad laments. The 45-year-old is now based in Turkey, but his family resides near Al-Omari Mosque in Shujaiyya, Gaza City.

"I attended every prayer there. It's a cherished ancient place my children love. I wonder why it was destroyed; does the mosque threaten the occupiers?"

He added that dozens of other mosques, like Al-Hasayna near Gaza's port, were razed. "These mosques hold our memories, especially during Ramadan. This war obliterated everything. I hope that Gaza will be rebuilt post-war, that I can relive these beautiful moments and revisit these places with my family."

The persistent targeting of mosques in Gaza has led many Palestinians to believe they are unsafe even during prayers. Despite the fear, a significant number refuse to cease attending mosques, expressing resilience against the attacks.

"I won't hesitate to go to the mosque. If I die there, it's a beautiful end to my life," Khaled Islim, 30, from Khan Yunis, asserts. "Mosques pose no danger. We'll rebuild them, raising the call to prayer amid the rubble. The scenes of the Quran torn and burned under debris are painful, reflecting the injustice Gaza faces."

The Ministry of Tourism and Antiquities condemned the destruction of the Omari Mosque as part of Israel's plan to erase Palestinian heritage.

It said the act violated international treaties, including the Hague Convention of 1907, the Fourth Geneva Convention of 1949 and UNESCO conventions on cultural property protection.

The Ministry of Tourism and Antiquities condemned the destruction of the Omari Mosque as part of Israel's plan to erase Palestinian heritage.

The ministry noted the mosque's historical roots dating back to a Byzantine monastery in the fifth century CE. It viewed the destruction as a "crime against the cultural heritage of the Palestinian people", symbolising their connection to the land.

The ministry highlighted other Israeli offences, including the destruction of archaeological sites like the old Gaza port, the Church of Porphyrius, the Jabalia Mosque, and numerous other historical buildings and museums. Urging international intervention, it appealed to UNESCO and the global community to compel Israel to "cease its aggression against the Palestinian people and their heritage", reaffirming that such acts wouldn't deter "the Palestinian people's determination for freedom and independence".

-

https://www.middleeasteye.net/news/gaza-war-israel-palestine-silences-historic-mosques

How Israel killed a disabled man

2 January 2024
SOURCE: THE ELECTRONIC INTIFADA

Israeli forces stormed Muhammad al-Salak's home in Shujaiya. He was arrested. When Khuloud, his wife, objected to his arrest, she was shot and killed ... He was killed several days later.

Muhammad al-Salak suffered enormously because of Israel's wars against Gaza. In the current war, he has been killed at the age of 48.

After Israel ordered residents of northern Gaza to evacuate their homes in October, Muhammad insisted on staying put. Muhammad — also known as Abu Al-Abd — was a resident of the Shujaiya neighborhood in Gaza City.

His neighbour and close friend Muhammad Abu Bayd left Shujaiya and went to Rafah, Gaza's southernmost city, following Israel's evacuation orders. Muhammad Abu Bayd did his best to keep in touch with Muhammad al-Salak, although it was very difficult given that internet access has been restricted for most people over the past few months. "I constantly asked him to leave his home and move south," Muhammad Abu Bayd said. "But he would not agree."

In December, Israeli forces stormed Muhammad al-Salak's home in Shujaiya. He was arrested. When Khuloud, his wife, objected to his arrest, she was shot and killed. Muhammad al-Salak was killed several days later, according to Muhammad Abu Bayd.

The al-Salak family was directly affected when Israel subjected Shujaiya to relentless shelling in July 2014. Muhammad's three children were massacred. Because of his injuries then, Muhammad lost his right leg. Close friend Muhammad Abu Bayd, who also lost one of his legs in 2014, recalled that "Muhammad al-Salak always talked about his children and said that he wanted to meet them again soon in heaven."

Muhammad Abu Bayd said, "When I lost my leg, I felt that my life was over." Yet the two Muhammads joined forces to set up a football team for amputees. They were also involved in a basketball team for wheelchair users.

... /

> "He filled the place with joy and we laughed a lot," Muhammad Abu Bayd, 37, says of his friend. "We felt that he would light up everything with his personality."

"He filled the place with joy and we laughed a lot," Muhammad Abu Bayd, 37, says of his friend. "We felt that he would light up everything with his personality."

"All the amputees felt that he was like a father to us," he added. "When one of us got angry during games and exercises, he tried to calm us down." Muhammad al-Salak used to work as a taxi driver. He originally bought his car in instalments and provided a taxi service to support his family.

After losing his leg, he would bring fellow amputees for drives on the seashore. "Despite everything Abu al-Abd [Muhammad al-Salak] lived through, he was a patient and wise man," Muhammad al-Bayd said. "I will miss him greatly."

-

https://electronicintifada.net/content/how-israel-killed-disabled-man/43486

War on Gaza: Displaced Palestinians find no shelter in Rafah

16 January 2024
SOURCE: MIDDLE EAST EYE (MEE)

Rasha Mansour's family fled south. "I took with me a blanket and enough bedding for the family and some other things," she said. Arriving in al-Mawasi, they found an overcrowded seaside wasteland.

Arriving at al-Mawasi, a town close to Rafah on Gaza's southern border with Egypt, 37-year-old Rasha Mansour found "nothing but sand and an empty place with no tents".

Mansour, her husband and their five children, left their home in central Gaza's al-Bureij refugee camp two weeks ago, after Israel ordered its residents to move to the adjacent Deir al-Balah, or to head south to Rafah, which is now home to more than a million displaced Palestinians.

With no space available at Deir al-Balah, Mansour told her husband she thought they should travel to Rafah, "so that we would not be forced to move anywhere again".

The war had already hit the family hard. A month in, Mansour told Middle East Eye that Israel was bombing their camp, despite assurances it was safe.

"During the second month of the war, I lost my younger brother Abdul Rahman and my uncle's family. The missiles fell on my uncle's house, next to us, and all my relatives in the building were killed. My uncle, his grandchildren, his daughters and my brother. My mother and father have been in Egypt for several months to treat my father. We are living in the most difficult circumstances without our parents."

Soon after, Mansour and her family fled south. "I took with me a blanket and enough bedding for the family and some other things," she said. Arriving in al-Mawasi, they found an overcrowded seaside wasteland.

"It was difficult to get a tent. I was very afraid to sit in the open without shelter with my three girls ... We stayed there for two days with great difficulty. I felt as if I was on the street. The place was

... /

> **In the last couple of days, Israel has rained down air strikes on Rafah, hitting homes sheltering displaced families and killing a reported 135 people.**

crowded with people. Some of them were making nylon tents for themselves, some were forced to sleep on the ground without a mattress."

Mansour's husband went looking for a tent and was told that some were being sold for as much as 2,000 shekels ($540), a price the family couldn't afford. "We made a tent of cloth and sat in it," the mother said. "We have left our homes, which used to be safe and warm, and now we are here in this empty place, in a tent of cloth. It is winter and very cold."

Around 1.9 million people have now been displaced from their homes in Gaza, with many heading south to Rafah and nearby al-Mawasi because these areas are considered safer than others — also this is where the Israeli military has told them to go.

Dire conditions

In a post on Telegram, Palestinian health ministry spokesman Ashraf al-Qudra said that infrastructure and medical services in Rafah could not handle the needs of an estimated 1.3 million displaced people.

In the last couple of days, Israel has rained down air strikes on Rafah, hitting homes sheltering displaced families and killing a reported 135 people. Rafah is the only Gaza border crossing not controlled by Israel, but according to the Wall Street Journal, Israeli officials have told Egypt they are planning a military operation on the Gaza side, where the displaced Palestinians are currently sheltering.

Despite hardships, Gaza refugees still seek end to "life-sapping" blockade

These Palestinians face dire conditions out in the open. "At any moment, rain could fall," Mansour said. "Thousands of citizens are in the street without a tent or shelter. The tent is not a solution. We need the war to stop, and we need to be allowed to return to our homes. We have lived through the Nakba of 1948, but what we are experiencing now is much more difficult."

In the city of Rafah, 40-year-old Rami Abu Quddus spends his days looking for somewhere he, his wife and three children can find shelter, after they were forced to leave Nuseirat camp in the middle of the Gaza Strip.

Rami Abu Quddus: "I have three children who have not recovered from the cold. We share appeals on social networking sites for a tent that is at least suitable for living, but there's nothing … I don't want to spend nearly $500 on a tent that will not protect us from the winter."

"The tent is not a good place to live," he told MEE. "I have three children who have not recovered from the cold. We share appeals on social networking sites for a tent that is at least suitable for living, but there's nothing. Everything requires money and is twice the price. The tent, food and drink and everything else are very expensive. I don't want to spend nearly $500 on a tent that will not protect us from the winter."

Abu Quddus said that some areas of al-Mawasi and other parts of Rafah had been bombed by Israel. "The Israeli army is not showing anyone mercy during this war. I cannot provide safety for my children. We, the displaced, are experiencing great suffering in Rafah. The army is pushing us there, knowing the city will explode due to the increase in population."

According to Abu Quddus and other displaced Palestinians in Rafah, there is not enough food in the city. "If I do not find any canned goods in the market, my family will never find anything to eat," he said. The city does not have the services and infrastructure to deal with the number of people that have fled to it and the humanitarian situation is deteriorating rapidly as a result.

"The Israeli army is still asking citizens to evacuate their residential areas in the city of Khan Yunis and go to Rafah," Abu Quddus said. "How long will we remain displaced like this? Are the tents we live in now acceptable?" His life and the lives of those around him are shattered, Abu Quddus talked to MEE about everything that had been lost to Israel's ongoing bombardment.

"I had dreams and a future for my children," he said. "I work as a teacher in a school and I had a beautiful daily routine. I want it back again. I want the war to end without losing anyone from my family. I miss my home, my neighbours, my camp." He paused. "I want to return to my life, to leave this tent that I made from some nylon, that does not protect us from the cold or the light. I want to leave the explosions at night, the deadly quiet during the day.

•

https://www.middleeasteye.net/news/israel-palestine-war-gaza-rafah-tents-shelter

The olive tree, symbol of Palestine and mute victim of Israel's war on Gaza

22 January 2024
SOURCE: AL JAZEERA

> To have to destroy one's own olive trees, one of the most enduring symbols of Palestine, is a wound that cuts deep and has left different-shaped scars in the hearts of the people.

Al-Fukhari, Gaza: Ahlam Saqr, 50, cried on the morning her sons started cutting branches off her olive trees to burn them for fires to cook, stay warm and heat water for bathing.

It was a matter of survival, she says, to enable the family to make it through the relentless Israeli bombing of Gaza. But that did not make it any easier to watch her four beloved trees being taken apart. "The house felt so empty. The trees had their place in the house and it became dark when they were gone. We have beautiful memories with them," she said.

Forced to lose "life companions"

Gaza is under a brutal Israeli bombardment and siege that has displaced most of its population and at the same time prevented fuel, gas for stoves, and other essentials from entering.

In the midst of human misery and crisis, a series of other tragedies have unfolded as families are forced to destroy their trees in order to have firewood for survival. To have to destroy one's own olive trees, one of the most enduring symbols of Palestine, is a wound that cuts deep and has left different-shaped scars in the hearts of the people who spoke to Al Jazeera.

Ahlam is not the only person in Gaza who has had to part with beloved trees just to be able to feed the family and keep everyone warm. In many homes, people are mourning having to destroy these living, breathing witnesses to family history. "I used to tell everyone that my trees have been my life companions. They've been there as I raised my children here; they've seen all the stages of our lives," Ahlam told Al Jazeera.

... /

> **By the time Khaled and his family fled Bani Suheila, half the trees were gone, cut down a little at a time for the family's needs or because the neighbours had come around begging for firewood to keep their own children warm and fed ...**

Khaled Baraka, 65, also grieves for his trees, but he is not actually sure what state they are in today because he was forced to flee from his home in Bani Suheila six weeks ago. "I was displaced ... when Israeli tanks entered the city of Khan Yunis, we were already having a hard time. My orchard and fields were right next to our house, and we had already started to burn branches," he said.

By the time Khaled and his family fled Bani Suheila, half the trees were gone, cut down a little at a time for the family's needs or because the neighbours had come around begging for firewood to keep their own children warm and fed.

"To make bread, you need a fire," he said bitterly. "How else was it supposed to happen? There were so many different types of trees. Guava, lemon, orange, and olive — they were all being cut down and I'm sure that once the occupation forces took the area they destroyed whatever was left."

Khaled inherited his trees from his father, he told Al Jazeera, and most of them are at least 70 years old. "These trees lived through my moments of joy and sadness," he said. "They know my secrets. When I was sad and worried, I would talk to the trees, take care of them ... but the war killed those trees."

"The trees were my friends"

Fayza Jabr, 60, has lived alone for 10 years, since her husband passed away. The couple had no children. About seven years before her husband's death, she planted two olive trees, a lemon tree and a clementine tree around her house and spent her time taking care of them and watching proudly as they matured and bore fruit.

"They were my friends, part of my life," Fayza said. "When a tree was in fruit, I'd call the neighbour's son, Abboud, who's 11. He would help me pick the fruit and prune trees that needed it. I didn't want to build a wall around my house so I could see the trees from inside and people walking by could enjoy the green."

"In mid-October, my brothers and sisters, their children and grandchildren were displaced to my home in Khan Yunis — more than 30 people in my little house, all of them needing food and bread. To manage that, we ended up having to use the trees to light fires."

The olive tree, symbol of Palestine and mute victim of Israel's war...

> "About a month after the harvest, I noticed that some of the branches were broken off so I asked my sisters about them. They told me they were forced to cut down the trees because there was no other solution."

At first, Fayza continued, it was possible to find bags of firewood in the market and to scrape together $30 to buy a bag that would last two days. But eventually, that supply ran out and her sisters would wake at dawn to scavenge for anything to feed the fire. All sorts of things were burned: fabric, plastic, even shoes.

"It was olive season at the end of October, so I asked my family to help me pick the olives, not knowing that that would be the farewell season for my trees. I think I was lucky to have been able to pick olives from my two trees. They're more than 17 years old. If they were my children, they'd be teenagers."

"About a month after the harvest, I noticed that some of the branches were broken off so I asked my sisters about them. They told me they were forced to cut down the trees because there was no other solution.

Now the garden is barren. We had to rip the trees up by the roots to use every last bit … I was sad. It's hard for me to cut down my trees, but I can't be angry because there are children in the house who need to eat."

The unspeakable richness of four trees

Ahlam moved to her house in al-Fukhari about 20 years ago, after Israeli forces destroyed the family's first home near Khan Yunis.

"UNRWA [United Nations Relief and Works Agency for Palestine Refugees] built these houses for us after we'd been displaced for a couple of years, me, my husband and our six children, moving from one temporary shelter to another. I was so happy, the new homes had space to plant trees and other things around them. There's nothing like plants to make a place feel comforting.

"When the municipality workers came around to give each home two olive trees, I sweet-talked them into giving me four instead, and I was so pleased with those four trees, it was like I owned a whole orchard."

"My daughter Israa could only study among these trees. She loved them, too. But since the beginning of the war, we've needed to light fires for cooking and it's a painful journey to search for wood.

… /

> **"We've lost so much in this war ... we grieve for these trees."**

We used everything, even plastic water pipes one day, and they smelled so bad that even the food tasted different ... My sons eventually suggested that we cut down trees. At first, they said only one tree and the war wouldn't last long. But the war didn't stop and now all the trees are gone," Ahlam said.

"We've lost so much in this war, it's not going to end — the trees were like our children," Khaled said, resigned. "We grieve for these trees, but there is no other solution."

-

https://www.aljazeera.com/features/2024/1/22/the-olive-tree-symbol-of-palestine-and-mute-victim-of-israels-war-on-gaza

Infections increase in Gaza

9 May 2024
SOURCE: THE ELECTRONIC INTIFADA

> I contracted pneumonia ... My body did not respond to the treatment for some time. It is highly likely that my immune system has been compromised due to poor nutrition.

Becoming ill during a war can be painful and disorientating. I know this from experience. Recently, I contracted pneumonia. I received some medicine through a clinic at a school that is now a shelter for displaced people. My body did not respond to the treatment for some time. It is highly likely that my immune system has been compromised due to poor nutrition. Eventually, I recovered. But I feel that I could easily become unwell again.

There are many others with similar stories. Husam is a 13-year-old. He and his family have been living recently in a tent. He spoke of suddenly feeling "very tired and weak." He lost his appetite and vomited frequently.

After tests at a hospital, Husam was diagnosed with hepatitis A, a virus transmitted by dirty water. Pools of sewage can be found around the tents where Husam's family and others have been living in Rafah, southern Gaza.

Husam had to stay in his tent for several weeks, with a nurse monitoring him. "I took medicine until I got better," he said. "But I do not feel in good health at all." The only water he has is polluted. He still drinks it so that he does not become dehydrated.

No protection

Following Israel's ground invasion of Rafah which began earlier this week, the city now has only one functioning hospital. Known as the Kuwaiti Hospital, it has just 16 beds. Speaking before the invasion occurred, Jamal al-Hams, a doctor in that hospital, said, "There are huge numbers of people displaced from all areas of the Gaza Strip concentrated in Rafah. They are living in very difficult conditions."

"There is no protection from viruses," he said. "And the food and nutrition available is not sufficient. Aid in the form of canned food does not meet people's needs."

... /

> **30,000 people are now sheltering at the European Hospital. Pools of sewage can be seen in its grounds and a great deal of garbage has accumulated ... There is a foul odour and a major problem with mosquitoes.**

Before this week's invasion began, the hospital was treating about 1,000 people with infectious diseases per day, according to al-Hams. That figure did not include people rushed to the hospital having just been injured in Israeli attacks.

The European Gaza Hospital — located in the southern city of Khan Yunis — is overwhelmed, too. Amal noticed that her son had a high temperature. After a few days, it was confirmed that he had hepatitis A. "I kept my child away from his siblings so that he didn't give the infection to them," Amal said. "I cannot do more for him."

Amal and her family are living in a tent at the hospital. "There is not enough water and there are no clean bathrooms," she said, adding that vast numbers of displaced people are using the same bathrooms. "If we survive the bombing, we will not survive disease and pollution," she said.

By some estimates, 30,000 people are now sheltering at the European Hospital. Pools of sewage can be seen in its grounds and a great deal of garbage has accumulated both inside and around the hospital. There is a foul odour and a major problem with mosquitos. The hospital's administration has warned that services could collapse at any moment.

•

https://electronicintifada.net/content/infections-increase-gaza/46301

Motherhood during genocide

23 May 2024
SOURCE: THE ELECTRONIC INTIFADA

> "They took me to the hospital, and I was crying hard. I wanted to see my son." She would never do so. He died along with his father in the blast.

What does it mean to be a mother in Gaza during genocide? For Ola Odeh, 36, from the city of Khan Yunis, it has meant losing her son and husband last October.

"My 9-year-old son Abdel Rahman was always asking me when we would go to my grandfather's house. Will there be a truce soon or not? I made him be patient and pray a lot for this war to stop, but I was afraid that the army would target entire residential areas," Odeh said. "He went downstairs with his father to sit with his grandfather and his cousins one day last October," she recalled. "My daughter Masa was playing in her room, and I was arranging clothes in my room. Suddenly there was a huge explosion. I felt like I was on the street. I hugged Masa and looked around."

"There were no stairs for me to go down, so I descended on piles of stones. They took me to the hospital, and I was crying hard. I wanted to see my son." She would never do so. He died along with his father in the blast. "Don't cry, mother," Odeh recalled Masa saying at the time. "The most important thing is that you are fine and I am with you."

"Losing Abdel Rahman was never easy," Odeh told The Electronic Intifada. "I feel like my heart is on fire. I cry bitterly every night. He was a very affectionate child. He listened to my words and responded to my requests ... I feel that the war made me hate life."

"The hardest thing is for a mother to lose her child," she says, echoing the thoughts of thousands of mothers whose children have been caught up in Israel's genocidal violence unleashed in Gaza.

Of the 14,500 children and 9,500 women reportely killed so far, the United Nations, citing Gaza's Health Ministry, has confirmed 7,797 child and 4,959 women fatalities in Gaza over the past nearly 8 months, saying there is incomplete documentation for the rest to make a final determination. UNICEF has called Gaza the world's "most dangerous place to be a child."

... /

> Hamid recalled (her son) Walid telling her that he wanted to go to Khan Yunis to sell okra. "He went … and he did not return. He came back to me covered in a shroud … my heart burned with a fire that made me lose the ability to speak."

Tears of a mother

"I still dream about his future. He was in the fifth grade," Odeh said of Abdel Rahman. "He had many interests. He was the first grandchild of my family. They loved him very much. I still see my father's tears and the pain in his heart over his loss." As she considers the future, Odeh added that she does not know how she will be both "a mother and father" to Masa. "The screams and tears of mothers have never been merciful," Odeh said.

Jawaher Hamid, 45, from Gaza City would likely agree. She lost her son Walid to deadly injuries suffered in a bombing in the Mawasi area west of Khan Yunis. "I was working in a school and cleaning its facilities in order to provide my children with what they needed. I was enduring extreme fatigue in order to help my son Walid to build a future for him," Hamid said, adding that she had been hoping to see Walid get married and welcome his children into the family.

Last October, Hamid said she and her seven children fled the intense bombing and left Gaza City, going to the Bureij camp in the middle of the Gaza Strip. "It was not easy. I was displaced to schools, which are the most difficult places to go to. I could hardly get water and food for my seven children. Walid and his brothers were helping me, but they could not bear this extreme fatigue of displacement," Hamid said. "When tanks stormed Bureij camp, we were displaced again to the city of Rafah."

Hamid recalled Walid telling her that he wanted to go to Khan Yunis to sell okra. "He went … and he did not return. He came back to me covered in a shroud," Hamid told The Electronic Intifada. "When the news came to me, my heart burned with a fire that made me lose the ability to speak … Walid, my eldest son, was martyred. His passing hurt my heart and his father's heart. I still have hope that everything I am experiencing will be a nightmare, and it will end," Hamid said.

Her son was buried in a cemetery in the city of Rafah. His sisters, who did not move to the south, did not have a chance to say goodbye to him, Hamid said. "They will not visit his grave because it is far from them, and when I return to Gaza City, his grave will be far from it."

> Alaa al-Qatrawi lost all four of her children together. "... Each one of them has a story of birth, upbringing, and care. Each one of them has a future and a dream that I hoped they could achieve. Is this possible for a mother to bear?"

Unjust world

Hamid said she had feared an Israeli military ground operation in Rafah, which would force her to be displaced a third time. "I was praying to God that this would not happen, but it happened," she said. "I was displaced while looking behind me at Walid's grave. I cried a lot. How would I be left with the sounds of tanks? Now I spend my time sitting by the sea. I cannot sit in the tent without Walid. I was hoping to endure all the hardships of war and not lose one of my children."

Alaa al-Qatrawi lost all four of her children together during the Israeli army's siege of their house next to Dar Al-Salam Hospital in Khan Yunis. Al-Qatrawi, 33, said she had been separated from her husband for about a year. The children lived with their father and visited her weekly.

After constantly communicating with them to make sure they were ok since the start of the genocide, al-Qatrawi said she suddenly lost contact with them in mid-December.

"The tanks were standing in front of their house. I waited a long time to check on them, but in March, I received news that the army had surrounded them and arrested their father and uncles and then bombed the house," al-Qatrawi said.

"I lost my four children. I had a dream of being able to travel with them to Dubai and build a life and a future there ... The occupation left my heart burning for my children," she said. "Each one of them has a story of birth, upbringing, and care. Each one of them has a future and a dream that I hoped they could achieve. Each one of them has friends and family who love them and miss them. Is this possible for a mother to bear? All of this in Gaza? Unfortunately, we are in an unjust world that has no humanity at all."

•

https://electronicintifada.net/content/motherhood-during-genocide/46586

Hunger is rapidly getting worse in Gaza

17 June 2024
SOURCE: THE ELECTRONIC INTIFADA

> Amani Labad's family can only eat one meal a day. "The army has bulldozed the agricultural lands and there are no vegetables in the markets ... And then comes the suffering of searching for food as well."

An especially bizarre example of propaganda has been published by the Israeli military over the past few days. Despite how it is perpetrating a genocide in Gaza, the army boasted of conducting "humanitarian aid efforts" throughout the current war. Palestinians have not witnessed any work by Israel that could accurately be categorised as "humanitarian."

Amani Labad has been in the northern part of Gaza since the war began. She has been uprooted many times. "I have been fighting all kinds of death," Amani said. "Death from violence and from severe hunger."

Her family can only eat one meal a day. "The army has bulldozed the agricultural lands and there are no vegetables in the markets," she said.

Amani is extremely worried that one or more of her four children could die from malnutrition. "I am very tired of being displaced from one place to another, searching for safety for my children," she said. "And then comes the suffering of searching for food as well."

Ahmad Kurd is from Jabaliya refugee camp in northern Gaza. "I have 10 grandchildren and I cannot bear to hear them crying from hunger," he said. "It is very painful ... How long will we remain in this situation?" he added. "We are all so tired."

For a number of months, the problems of hunger and malnutrition were more acute in northern Gaza than in the south. Yet the World Food Programme has warned that the situation in southern Gaza is "quickly deteriorating."

Israel's invasion of Rafah has meant that the crossing between that city and Egypt is closed. Far less food is entering Gaza as a result.

... /

> "I have a child with very weak immunity ... He craves fruit but I am unable to provide it."

Rami Labda is from Khan Yunis, another city in southern Gaza. "They have closed the crossing and left us to die," he said. "I have a child with very weak immunity because of malnutrition," Rami added. "He craves fruit and asks me for some every day but I am unable to provide it." Echoing a widespread view, Rami said, "Why do they not want the war to stop? Sometimes we feel like we are going to lose our minds because of what we are going through."

•

https://electronicintifada.net/content/hunger-rapidly-getting-worse-gaza/47166

When Israel attacked hungry children

19 July 2024
SOURCE: THE ELECTRONIC INTIFADA

> A child named Abd al-Rahman was hungry. His mother was unable to cook anything for him. So she told him to head for a communal kitchen in al-Mawasi, where food was being distributed ... He is still alive after the massacre, though he required an amputation. Many others were killed.

Yasmine al-Akkad had given birth a few weeks earlier. When she heard a loud explosion last Saturday, she immediately grabbed her baby. Then she lifted her other daughter — a 2-year-old — and began running through al-Mawasi in southern Gaza.

Yasmine survived the massacre in which more than 90 others were killed. But she is deeply traumatised by what she witnessed. "The worst thing I saw was the body of my brother-in-law on a tree," she said. "It was cut in two."

A child named Abd al-Rahman was hungry. His mother was unable to cook anything for him. So she told him to head for a communal kitchen in al-Mawasi, where food was being distributed. Abd al-Rahman is still alive after the massacre — though he required an amputation. Many others who had joined him in the queue for food were killed.

A mother was preparing food for her children, when suddenly she heard explosions. "Everything went black," she said. "I could not see anything because there was so much smoke and dust." There were more explosions. The woman began screaming and searching for her family. First, she found the body of her baby niece. All around the area where she was living in a tent, she saw numerous dead bodies. She went searching for her husband and her two children, aged 7 and 9. She was not able to find them and assumes they have been killed. "What did these hungry children do to be killed in such a brutal way?" the woman asked.

Earthquake

Maha Ahmad described Israel's bombardment as so heavy that "the area shook like there had been an earthquake." Many of the dead were in so many pieces that their surviving relatives either could not identify them or had trouble doing so.

... /

> "We have now lost more than 10 people in our family since the beginning of this war."

Maha's home in the city of Khan Yunis has been destroyed during the current genocidal war. She had been displaced to Rafah, Gaza's southernmost city. When Israel undertook a ground invasion of Rafah in May, it designated al-Mawasi a "safe zone." "The whole world began to know al-Mawasi as a safe area but unfortunately it isn't," Maha added. "It has become the most dangerous area for the displaced."

Rami Labda was searching for water in al-Mawasi on Saturday when Israel's attack began. He rushed to check on his family's tent and was reassured that it was empty. His family had planned a trip to the sea that day. People in nearby tents had not been spared. "I found three of my neighbours injured and another one killed," Rami said.

Amal Akar was displaced from an area east of Khan Yunis to al-Mawasi a few weeks ago. On Saturday, her nephew Fayez had gone shopping when Israel attacked. "Everyone started phoning to check on him," Amal said. "But he did not reply."

After approximately an hour, Amal heard that Fayez had been injured. She and others in the family went to look for him at Nasser Medical Complex in Khan Yunis. "The scene there was frightening," she said. "There were mothers screaming and doctors running around, trying to save the patients."

Amal learned that Fayez had been bleeding heavily. A doctor was attending to him when he died. "It was a great shock," she said. "We have now lost more than 10 people in our family since the beginning of this war."

"The repeated targeting of al-Mawasi is frightening all the displaced people there," she added … "People want to leave the area but they cannot find other places to go. There has been huge destruction in all areas of Gaza."

•

https://electronicintifada.net/content/when-israel-attacked-hungry-children/47821

Netzarim corridor: Israel's "axis of death" for Palestinians

24 December 2024
SOURCE: MIDDLE EAST EYE (MEE)

> When a rumour spread that displaced Palestinians could travel from Southern Gaza back to the north, Sabreen Lashin was one of the first to attempt to return home. At the Netzarim corridor checkpoint Israeli soldiers ... rejected her pleas to return home, and began shooting at people.

Earlier this year, when a rumour spread that Palestinians could travel from southern Gaza to the north, Sabreen Lashin was one of the first to attempt to return home.

But, much to her disappointment, the mother from Gaza City's al-Shati refugee camp was blocked by Israeli forces occupying the so-called Netzarim corridor, or the "axis of death" as Palestinians refer to it.

Fed up with the miserable life of displacement she had endured in southern Gaza for a year and three months, she refused to give up. Along with five other women, she attempted to explain to the soldiers the harsh living conditions in southern Gaza. There, she had been displaced 14 times, each time seeking safety from Israeli bombardment, but to no avail.

"My children can't find work, and I can't afford the medication I need," the 44-year-old tells Middle East Eye. "The constant displacement, hunger, bombings, and humiliation in the south eventually pushed me to make the difficult decision to return to the north, despite the risks."

At the checkpoint in the Netzarim corridor, some Israeli soldiers listened to her, while others remained silent. All of them rejected her pleas to return to her home. Without warning, she says, Israeli forces began shooting at people who had approached the corridor, hoping to return home.

"One of the women, a 35-year-old, was shot twice — once in the back and once below her chest," Lashin told MEE. She clutched Lashin's arm, pleading with her not to leave her behind for the soldiers to find.

... /

> **Lashin had no choice but to drag the shot woman back toward the south ... A tank rolled over the area, threatening to run over the woman. A soldier stepped out and told Lashin to leave the woman behind, but she refused. "She's still alive," Lashin insisted.**

Lashin had no choice but to drag the woman back toward the south, as the others fled in fear from the sound of gunfire. As they moved, a tank rolled over the area, threatening to run over the woman.

A soldier stepped out and told Lashin to leave the woman behind, but she refused. "She's still alive," Lashin insisted.

She eventually managed to drag the woman along the road until she reached a group of young men, who helped take the wounded woman to al-Awda hospital in Nuseirat. But tragically, she did not survive.

This was one of 12 attempts Lashin made to return to her home in northern Gaza, and it likely won't be the last. "Each time, I narrowly escape death, but I refuse to give up," she says. "I keep hoping that one day the soldiers will show some mercy and let me return."

At the Netzarim corridor, she adds, the area is filled with military jeeps and tanks, while drones hover overhead, targeting anyone who approaches. But the risk of dying while attempting to return home is better than staying displaced in the south, she tells MEE.

"I still dream of returning home," she adds. "I want to set up a tent on the rubble of my house and live with my children, rather than enduring the humiliation of displacement in the south."

An axis of death

Lashin is one of the hundreds of thousands of internally displaced Palestinians whom Israel has been blocking from returning to their homes since the war began last year. Ahead of its invasion of Gaza in late October 2023, the Israeli military forced more than one million Palestinians in northern Gaza to head south under heavy bombing.

The military promised safety in the south and stated that the relocation would be temporary. However, the hundreds of thousands who complied have been bombed in the south, including when in schools, makeshift tents, hospitals, and other shelters.

Meanwhile, Israeli troops invaded the so-called Netzarim Corridor, a 6km stretch of land south of Gaza City that divides the strip into its northern and southern parts. It stretches from the Israeli boundary with Gaza City in the east to the Mediterranean Sea.

> Mohammed Hajjo: "They forced me to throw away everything I had — clothes, supplies — and even took my phone. I saw a large hole filled with items from other displaced families, discarded as though they didn't matter ... They made me take off my clothes, I thought they would arrest me, but in the morning, they let me go, naked."

The Netzarim route is now reportedly 7km wide and contains military bases. It is used by Israeli forces to monitor and control the movement of Palestinians between northern and southern Gaza and to launch military operations.

Mohammed Hajjo, from Sheikh Radwan in Gaza City, initially refused to leave northern Gaza. His wife and children moved south at the onset of the war, but he chose to stay and guard the house, assuming their absence in the south would be brief. But when the war dragged on with no end in sight and severe hunger reached southern Gaza, he decided to cross the Netzarim corridor and move south to help his family. "I took many clothes for my children because the cold in the tents was unbearable. I also brought clothes for my wife and many other things," Hajjo told MEE.

His journey was long and filled with fear. "I walked for a long time along the coast, constantly fearing being sniped or arrested," the 32-year-old father recalled. When he reached the Netzarim checkpoint, the soldiers stopped him. "They forced me to throw away everything I had — clothes, supplies — and even took my phone. I saw a large hole filled with items from other displaced families, discarded as though they didn't matter ... There were many soldiers, tanks, cameras, and scanning devices everywhere. The landscape had changed so much, but I wasn't focused on that. I was focused only on getting out of there safely."

The soldiers held him overnight. "They made me take off my clothes, took everything from me, and asked many pointless questions — why I had fled south now, and not earlier. I thought they would arrest me, but in the morning, they let me go, naked."

A young man saw him on the road and helped him put on some clothes, before he eventually reached his family in Khan Yunis. Despite the relief of reuniting with his family, the ordeal still weighed heavily on him. "I was heartbroken because they made me throw away everything my family desperately needed. We had already suffered so much humiliation and degradation during the war. This place, Netzarim, is an axis of death, not just a checkpoint."

... /

> It has been designated a "kill zone" by the Division 252 (IDF) commander ... allowing soldiers to shoot "anyone who enters". Those killed are posthumously branded "terrorists," even if they are children.

Gone without a trace

Hajjo was one of the few lucky ones who managed to reach the Netzarim corridor and come out alive. Last week, a *Ha'aretz* (newspaper) investigation revealed that hundreds of Palestinians, including children, have been indiscriminately shot dead by Israeli soldiers at the Netzarim Corridor.

It has been designated a "kill zone" by the Division 252 commander, according to a senior officer, allowing soldiers to shoot "anyone who enters". Those killed are posthumously branded "terrorists," even if they are children.

The boundaries of the zone were largely arbitrary and extended "as far as a sniper can see," another member of the division told *Ha'aretz*. "We're killing civilians there, who are then counted as terrorists," he added.

Another soldier referred to a military spokesperson announcing that their division had killed more than 200 "militants" in Gaza. But of those 200 casualties, only 10 were confirmed to be known Hamas operatives, he said.

Though many are killed, others are arbitrarily detained at the checkpoint and forcibly disappeared. Intisar al-Attar, 58, lost one of her sons in an Israeli bombardment at the start of the war, forcing her to flee Gaza City south with the rest of her family. But after months of displacement, her other son, Sami, decided to make the dangerous journey north in the hopes of returning home. That was three months ago, and al-Attar has yet to hear from him. "I do not know anything about him. Was he martyred or arrested? I do not know," she told MEE.

Attar says she stands nearby, hoping someone will bring her the reassurance she desperately needs regarding the fate of her son. But the recent reports of arbitrary killings of Palestinians near the corridor have only added to her fears. "The soldiers' statements in the news are frightening. They say they shoot anyone who approaches that area," she said.

Attar says she stands nearby, hoping someone will bring her the reassurance she desperately needs regarding the fate of her son. But the recent reports of arbitrary killings of Palestinians near the corridor have only added to her fears.

"I hope the war stops so that I can go to the Netzarim area and search for my son. If he's dead, I want to bury him. If they've arrested him, I want to reassure myself about him … My heart has been burning since he left me," she says with tears in her eyes.

•

https://www.middleeasteye.net/news/netzarim-corridor-israels-axis-death-palestinians

"Broken": Domestic violence impacts women and children in Gaza

25 December 2024
SOURCE: AL JAZEERA

> "As a displaced family, the loss of privacy has added a whole new layer of pressure. I don't want to say that my life was perfect before the war, but I was able to express what was inside me in conversation with my husband."

Khan Yunis, Gaza — The face of Samar Ahmed, 37, shows clear signs of exhaustion. It is not just because she has five children, nor that they have been displaced several times since the start of Israel's brutal war on Gaza 14 months ago and are now living in cramped, cold conditions in a makeshift tent in the al-Mawasi area of Khan Yunis. Samar is also a victim of domestic violence and has no way to escape her abuser in the cramped conditions of this camp.

Two days ago, her husband beat her around the face leaving her with a swollen cheek and a blood spot in her eye. Her eldest daughter clung to her all night following that attack, which happened in front of the children.

Samar does not want to break up her family — they have already been forced to move from Gaza City to the Shati camp in Rafah and now to Khan Yunis — and the children are young. Her eldest, Laila, is just 15. She also has 12-year-old Zain, 10-year-old Dana, Lana, seven, and Adi, five, to think about.

On the day that Al Jazeera visits her, she is trying to keep her two younger girls occupied with schoolwork. Sitting together in the small tent, which is made from rags, the three have spread out some notebooks around them. Little Dana is huddled up close to her mother, seemingly wanting to give her support. Her younger sister is crying from hunger and Samar seems at a loss as to how to help them both.

As a displaced family, the loss of privacy has added a whole new layer of pressure. "I lost my privacy as a woman and a wife in this place. I don't want to say that my life was perfect before the war, but I was able to express what was inside me in conversation with my husband. I could scream without anyone hearing me," Samar says. "I could control my children more in my home.

.../

> A loud argument between a husband and wife drifts through from the tent next door. Samar's face turns red with embarrassment and sadness as bad language fills the air. She does not want her children to hear this.

Here, I live in the street and the cover of concealment has been removed from my life."

A loud argument between a husband and wife drifts through from the tent next door. Samar's face turns red with embarrassment and sadness as bad language fills the air. She does not want her children to hear this.

Her instinct is to tell the children to go out and play, but Laila is washing dishes in a small bowl of water and the argument next door brings her own problems back into sharp focus. "Every day, I suffer from anxiety because of the disagreements with my husband. Two days ago, it was a great shock for me that he hit me in this way in front of my children. All our neighbours heard my screams and crying and came to calm the situation between us."

"I felt broken," Samar says, worried the neighbours will think she is to blame — that her husband shouts so much because she is a bad wife. "Sometimes, when he screams and curses, I stay quiet so that those around us think he's screaming at someone else. I try to preserve my dignity a little," she says.

Samar tries to pre-empt her husband's anger by attempting to solve the problems facing the family herself. She visits the aid workers every day to ask for food. She believes it is the pressures of the war that have made her husband this way. Before the war, he worked in a small carpentry shop with a friend and this kept him busy. There were fewer arguments.

Now, she says: "Because of the severity of the disagreements between me and my husband, I wanted a divorce. But I hesitated for the sake of my children."

Samar goes to psychological support sessions with other women, to try to release some of the negative energy and anxiety building inside her. It helps her to hear that she is not alone. "I hear the stories of many women and I try to console myself with what I am going through, through their experiences."

As she talks, Samar gets up to start preparing food. She is fretting about when her husband will return and whether there will be enough to eat. A plate of beans with cold bread is all she can rustle up right now. She cannot light the fire because there is no gas.

> "This is not a life. I can't comprehend what I'm living. I'm trying to adapt to these difficult circumstances, but I cannot. I've turned from a practical and professional man into a man who gets so angry all the time."

Suddenly, Samar goes silent, fearful that a voice outside belongs to her husband. It does not. She asks her daughters to sit down and look at their maths problems. She whispers: "He went out shouting at Adi. I hope he is in a good mood."

Later on, Samar's husband, Karim Badwan, 42, sits beside his daughters, crammed inside the small tent they are living in. He is despairing. "This is not a life. I can't comprehend what I'm living. I'm trying to adapt to these difficult circumstances, but I cannot. I've turned from a practical and professional man into a man who gets so angry all the time."

Karim says he is deeply ashamed that he has hit his wife on several occasions since the war began. "I hope the war ends before my wife's energy runs out and she leaves me," he says. "My wife is a good woman, so she tolerates what I say." A tear rolls down Samar's bruised face as she listens.

Karim says he knows what he is doing is wrong. Before the war, he never dreamed he would be capable of harming her. "I had friends who used to beat their wives. I used to say: 'How does he sleep at night?' Unfortunately, now I do it."

"I did it more than once, but the hardest time was when I left a mark on her face and eye. I admit that this is a huge failure in terms of self-control," Karim says, his voice trembling. "The pressures of war are great. I left my home, my work and my future and I am sitting here in a tent, helpless in front of my children. I can't find a job and when I leave the tent, I feel that if I talk to anyone I will lose my temper."

Karim knows his wife and children have endured a great deal. "I apologise to them for my behaviour, but I keep doing it. I maybe need medication, but my wife does not deserve all this from me. I am trying to stop so that she doesn't have to leave me."

Samar's despair is compounded by the loss of her own family who she left in the north to flee the bombing with her husband and his family. Now, she is desperately lonely.

... /

> Laila: "My father shouts at me a lot. Sometimes he hits my sisters. My mother cries all night and wakes up with swollen eyes from sadness." Laila sits in her bed for long hours thinking about their lives before the war. "I try to be strong for my mother."

Her greatest fear is that she will completely burn out and become unable to care for her family, as she worries her husband already has. The responsibility for finding water and food, caring for the children, and thinking about their future, has all taken its toll and she lives in a constant state of fear.

"Trying to be strong for my mother"

As the eldest child, Laila is developing severe anxiety from the fighting between her father and mother and she fears for her mother. She says: "My father and mother quarrel every day. My mother suffers from a strange nervous state. Sometimes she shouts at me for no reason. I try to bear it and understand her condition so that I don't lose her. I do not like seeing her in this state, but the war did all of this to us."

Laila still sees Karim as a good father and blames the world for allowing this brutal war to go on for so long. "My father shouts at me a lot. Sometimes he hits my sisters. My mother cries all night and wakes up with swollen eyes from sadness over what we are living." She sits in her bed for long hours thinking about their lives before the war and her plans to study English. "I try to be strong for my mother."

"Unimaginable conditions"

The family is not alone. In Gaza, there has been a marked rise in domestic violence with many women attending psychological support sessions offered by aid workers in clinics.

Kholoud Abu Hajir, a psychologist, has met many victims since the start of the war at clinics in the displacement camps. However, she fears there are far more who are too ashamed to talk about it.

"There is a great secrecy and fear among the women of talking about it," she says. "I have received many cases of violence away from group sessions — women who want to talk about what they are suffering and ask for help."

> The number of divorces has risen — many between spouses who have been separated by the Israeli armed corridor between the north and the south. The war has taken a terrible toll on women and children, particularly.

Living in a constant state of instability and insecurity, enduring repeated displacement and being forced to live in tents crowded very closely together have deprived women of privacy, leaving them with nowhere to turn.

"There is no comprehensive psychological treatment system," Abu Hajir tells Al Jazeera. "We only work in emergency situations. The cases we deal with really require multiple sessions, and some of them are difficult cases where women need protection. There are very severe cases of violence that have reached sexual assault, and this is a dangerous thing."

The number of divorces has risen — many between spouses who have been separated by the Israeli armed corridor between the north and the south. The war has taken a terrible toll on women and children, particularly, Abu Hajir says.

Nevin al-Barbari, 35, a psychologist, says it is impossible to give children in Gaza the support they need in these conditions. "Unfortunately, what children are experiencing during the war cannot be described. They need very long psychological support sessions. Hundreds of thousands of children have lost their homes, lost a family member, and many of them have lost their entire family."

Being forced to live in difficult — and sometimes violent — family circumstances has made life immeasurably worse for many. "There is very clear and widespread family violence among the displaced in particular … Children's psychological and behavioural states have been affected very negatively. Some children have become very violent and hit other children violently."

Recently, al-Barbari came across the case of a 10-year-old child who had hit another with a stick, causing severe injury and bleeding. "When I met this child, he kept crying," she says. "He thought that I would punish him. When I asked him about his family, he told me that his mother and father have a big fight every day and his mother goes to her family's tent for days. He said he missed his home, his room and the way his family used to be. This child is a very common example of thousands of children."

… /

"It will be a long road to recovery for these children", al-Barbari says. "There are no schools to occupy them. Children are forced to bear great responsibilities, filling water containers and waiting in long lines for food aid. There are no recreational areas for them."

"There are so many stories that we do not know about, that these children are living every day," he said. "They miss their homes, their rooms and the way their families used to be. This is very common for thousands of children."

-

https://www.aljazeera.com/news/2024/12/25/i-am-broken-the-women-enduring-domestic-violence-amid-israel-war-on-gaza

I cannot believe our nightmare is over in Gaza

18 January 2025
SOURCE: SLATE MAGAZINE

Since the first moment of the war I have been thinking about when it will end … When I spoke to people during interviews and produced video stories and news articles, the only dream and wish expressed was for the war to stop and for everyone to return home.

Since the first moment of the war, I have been thinking about when it will end — whether it will be in two days, or in a week, or perhaps much longer. I was following the news closely from the start, and soon after it began, they were talking about the complexities and difficulties of changing the situation. It wasn't long before I entered a state of fear, one that often prevented me from hoping that the war would ever stop.

Since October 2023, we have lived through difficulties that cannot be described, but with each passing month, we would say that this might be the last month of the war — that we will start the next month in peace. Fifteen months passed, and every day I was waiting for that moment: the moment when they would announce the ceasefire. Each time I called my family and friends, everyone's only wish was for it to happen. When I spoke to people during interviews and produced video stories and news articles, the only dream and wish expressed was for the war to stop and for everyone to return home.

My students also always talked about their hope for the war's end, about their longing to return to their homes and schools. Many times, I felt that this wish was so simple, to live in peace and security, for the killing and destruction to stop — but how? When? Who would be able to stop this stubborn horror? All those months, the weight of these questions tired our minds. The question of when weighed on top of the extreme fatigue I felt from the successive crises of war: the lack of water and electricity, then the lack of food and endurance of famine, and then my injury last August during an Israeli airstrike. Facing death and surviving that incident, I didn't want to lose hope.

Before the bombing, I used to speak regularly with an old classmate, and she would assure me the war would end: "Every story has a

… /

> **News spread throughout Gaza about the possibility of an agreement. During that week, I felt that there was hope, that this long suffering might finally end.**

beginning and an end, and the war has a near end", she would say. She had heart disease, a severe condition, and as a result she chose not to make the difficult journey from the north to the south. She chose to stay, and she wound up losing both her home and her place of work. She endured through the famine, and she escaped death several times. But in the end, it was too much. The bombs did not kill her, not directly, but her heart couldn't take it all. One day it just stopped — and she didn't make it. She didn't survive to see this day. If she could hear me now, I would want her to know that she gave me hope, and that she was right.

Month after month I would walk through the streets, and the people around me would wonder: What happened in the negotiations? Did the two parties agree to stop the war? Did a powerful country intervene that could force them to end this? Month after month, I was pleading: Who will save these people from the war machine, from the bombing and killing that never stops? Whenever I took a taxi, the drivers and other passengers only ever talked about their memories from before the war and their hope to return to that life. Two million people in Gaza shared this wish.

A week ago, President-elect Donald Trump repeated his statements about the need to reach a ceasefire before he takes office. That was when the negotiations began to intensify and become more serious. News spread throughout Gaza about the possibility of an agreement. During that week, I felt that there was hope, that this long suffering might finally end. I became more positive, and I tried to support my friends and colleagues around me: It's coming. The war will end soon. Really. The displaced people in various areas of the southern Gaza Strip came out of their tents, shouting and chanting, demanding a ceasefire. This time, all the reports said that the seriousness of the negotiations was different.

On Wednesday evening, I could not believe the news: The negotiations had succeeded, the ceasefire would actually happen, and it would start on Sunday. A dam broke. My eyes filled with tears — from joy or sadness or fear, I do not know. My family was very happy. These have been 15 difficult and heavy months for everyone. Everyone I know supported this agreement. They lived through periods of despair and shorter periods of hope, again and again.

> We do not want to lose anyone else in the final moments of the war. We have endured a lot together ... and overcome many hardships. We want to survive together, to continue life and to know moments of freedom and safety.

We sat watching the celebrations of the displaced people. Then the neighbours and children came out chanting, clapping, and singing for freedom. All wanted the three days ahead to end so that Sunday would come and the war would stop. I wished the same: to close my eyes and wake up on Sunday, the war already over.

But it is not over yet. These past few days have been heavy. The bombing has not stopped. We do not want to lose anyone else in the final moments of the war. We have endured a lot together. We have endured a lot of pain and overcome many hardships. We want to survive together, to continue life and to know moments of freedom and safety. I called my friends and colleagues to hear their voices of joy. But everyone has a mix of feelings. Some are consumed with fear and anxiety about returning to the north and seeing that their homes have been destroyed.

My colleague Enas bought a house a few months before the war. I went to visit her in June of 2023, before it all began. I toured her house, and she was so happy with it, enthusing over its details. She moved from the difficult life of the Jabaliya camp to the most upscale residential area in Gaza City. But her joy with the new house was arrested. The war came, and it forced her to move farther north. She used to talk to me every day about when the war would stop. When they announced the ceasefire, she told me about how worried she was, wondering whether she would be able to see her beautiful house again, or if it will have become something else entirely. If it is damaged, what will I do with it? Would I rebuild it again, or would another war just come and destroy it? Still, she too is happy that the war is ending, that the awful sounds of bombing and warplanes of all kinds will stop.

Another colleague, Bayan, is also from the north, but her story is sadder. She was displaced to the south with her two daughters. During the war, she lost one of them, and now she will return home with only one. When I talked to her, I consoled her: The war was over, and finally, she would return home, her surviving daughter at her side. I found her very strong. The news made her happy. When she gets back to the north, she will meet her husband, whom she left there and has not seen for 15 months.

... /

> **We need peace and security, because we are a people who have not lived a moment in either, for more than just this war — for years.**

And she will finally see me again. She says that she misses me and wants to hug me for the sake of freedom, and to celebrate the end of the war.

As for myself, I will take some time to rest. I need my mind to rest from constantly thinking about survival. I need my heart to rest from the intense fear of hearing any sudden sound. I have become more nervous, and I look for any quiet time I can find.

I have been running away to sleep, to try to end the days of war for myself, despite waking up screaming at every sound of bombing. Now I can actually rest; I can move around without fear; I won't have to be nervous when one of my family members leaves. We will try to rebuild our lives again. It will take a long time, but we will do it. My sister and her children are so happy that the war will stop. Rital, my 5-year-old nephew, asks if the bombing will really end, and if we will rebuild our house again.

"I want my room to be beautiful."

We still have these dreams, and we still have hope that the coming days will be better. I will return to my school in the north and meet my colleagues and students, and I will hug them a lot. We will cry a lot for those we have lost — students and colleagues from that beautiful school. We need peace and security, because we are a people who have not lived a moment in either, for more than just this war — for years. The successive wars have hurt us too much. We have lost too many loved ones, too many places, too many memories. Perhaps this will be the last war, at last.

•

https://slate.com/news-and-politics/2025/01/ceasefire-gaza-israel-hamas-palestinian-personal-essay.html

Beatings, diseases, humiliation: A Palestinian doctor's year in Israeli jails

18 February 2025
SOURCE: +972 MAGAZINE

> Mahmoud Abu Shahada was one of 70 medical staff arrested, along with dozens of patients, during Israel's invasion of the Nasser Medical Complex in Khan Yunis ... Israel detained him for nearly a year, subjecting him to persistent abuse and forcing him to live in harsh conditions.

Amid the haze of the Israeli army's manifold raids on medical facilities in the Gaza Strip over the past year and a half, it is easy to lose sight of their human impact. The story of Dr. Mahmoud Abu Shahada, the chief of orthopaedics at Nasser Medical Complex in Khan Yunis, helps to reveal their arbitrary brutality and cruelty.

Mahmoud Abu Shahada was one of 70 medical staff arrested along with dozens of patients on Febuary 17, 2024, during Israel's invasion of the hospital. The arrests were the culmination of a nearly month-long seige on Gaza's second largest medical facility, where troops fired on the hospital and its courtyard, demolished of the complex's northern wall, targeted its water tanks, and cut off electricity.

His lawyer says Abu Shahada had not taken any part in the fighting, but Israel detained him for nearly a year, subjecting him to persistent abuse and forcing him to live in harsh conditions. Following an appeal to Israel's Supreme Court, he was finally released on 10 January 2025. He spoke to +972 shortly after. This interview has been edited for length and clarity.

Please introduce yourself

"My name is Mahmoud Abu Shahada and I'm 42 years old. I work at Nasser Medical Complex as a consultant and have headed the orthopaedic department since 2017. I have worked in the Health Ministry since 2009. Like all the people of Gaza, I have lived through many wars, and I treated patients whom Israeli forces had wounded during the Great March of Return protests. But nothing was as intense, brutal, and barbaric as this war, with so much displacement and destruction.

… /

> "On December 5, 2023 the ground invasion began in Khan Yunis. It was very difficult for me because I was away from the house as the Israeli tanks were approaching it. My family had difficulty evacuating that morning ... "

Tell us about your life before the war, and how it changed after October 7.

Before October 7, we lived a quiet life. From the morning until 2 p.m. I would be at the hospital working. Then, I would spend some time with my family. From late afternoon until evening I would work in my private clinic, except for Thursdays, which was my day off. That day was for my children and my wife and it was always busy; we would go out and have dinner outside the house. It was a beautiful day that we always looked forward to. We would release the negative energy and pressures of work and life.

After October 7, I was working a lot in the hospital. We prepared the medical teams to receive the wounded. My children were at home near the southern branch of the Islamic University, and I used to go and visit them twice a week.

On December 5, 2023, however, the ground invasion began in Khan Yunis. It was very difficult for me because I was away from the house as the Israeli tanks were approaching it. My family had difficulty evacuating that morning, but they took up residence at the European Hospital [just outside the city].

I continued my work at the Nasser Complex, and once a week I would go and visit my family. I would spend one day with them and then return to my work in rotation with the doctors who were also visiting their families at the European Hospital for the day. This situation continued until the beginning of February, when Israel began besieging Nasser Hospital, and my children insisted on being close to me.

Can you describe what happened in the lead-up to Israel's raid?

On the evening of February 15, Israeli forces targeted one of the rooms in the orthopaedics department next to my office. The entire hospital was in a state of fear. The army ordered us to evacuate the displaced people and patients who were able to walk, leaving only the doctors and immobile patients ... It was very difficult for me to say goodbye to my children, but I was very afraid about what would happen to them if they stayed.

> "The soldiers lined up all of the doctors ... and ordered us to take off our clothes. They checked our identity, blindfolded us, handcuffed us, and led us into the basement of one of the buildings, where they humiliated, insulted, and severely beat us ... we were naked and they sprayed us with cold water ... "

They left with my wife at dawn through the humanitarian corridor. I will not forget those rainy moments in which we parted and did not know each other's fate.

What happened on the day of your arrest?

The soldiers lined up all of the doctors in front of the administration building and ordered us to take off our clothes. They checked our identity, blindfolded us, handcuffed us, and led us into the basement of one of the buildings, where they humiliated, insulted, and severely beat us.

From Friday afternoon until Saturday morning, we endured a difficult night of beating and abuse. The weather was cold and we were naked and they sprayed us with cold water. At dawn, they loaded us into large open trucks and transported us to detention centres. They were driving fast and I could feel the truck shaking from the roughness of the road.

During the transport, they sprayed us again with cold water and beat us, until we reached the detention centres. They dragged us out of the trucks in a very humiliating way and beat us again, before once more verifying our identities and dressing us in pants and a pullover.

The detention centres were enclosed by barbed wire and chains, resembling cages. They put us in holding cells and each one had a mattress no thicker than a centimetre that we sat on all day, still handcuffed and blindfolded. For two months, we were constantly transferred to interrogation rooms, while being subjected to humiliation and torture.

We were then transferred to Ofer Camp, which consisted of many rooms containing approximately 15 to 20 prisoners each. Our hands were cuffed and only after two full days did they remove our blindfolds. The beating and abuse continued. Two or three times each day, masked soldiers would enter and move us from room to room, beating and humiliating us, while taking all the food and water and throwing it away outside.

... /

> "After three months, we were transferred to the Negev Prison [Ketziot], where we faced more beating and abuse. I suffered from severe bruises in the chest area and broken ribs, and wounds on my hands from being shackled ... We experienced illness, fatigue, and weakness to the point that we couldn't stand and would get dizzy and lightheaded."

What was your experience like in prison?

I spent about three months in Ofer. They gave us three meals a day: four small pieces of bread and a spoonful of yogurt or half a spoonful of jam. It was useless food. Their goal might have been to keep us alive, and not much else. As for personal hygiene, it was very bad. They would turn on the water in the bathrooms once every two weeks to shower without soap, shampoo, toothpaste, or a toothbrush. We suffered a lot when we went to the bathroom.

After three months, we were transferred to the Negev Prison [Ketziot], where we faced more beating and abuse. I suffered from severe bruises in the chest area and broken ribs, and wounds on my hands from being shackled.

When I arrived at [Ketziot], the other detainees were suffering with skin diseases, pus, and severe infections. After a while, the infections spread to us. We experienced illness, fatigue, and weakness to the point that we couldn't stand and would get dizzy and lightheaded.

The worst thing was showering and personal hygiene. They would cut off the water for long hours, including the drinking water. The water in the showers was cold. We were forced to use it to maintain personal hygiene, but we suffered from diseases.

We would receive news from the new detainees arriving from Gaza. They told us that the war was ongoing, the destruction and killing had increased many times over, and there was famine. We felt very sad for our families and prayed that the war would end and that we and our families would be safe.

When other detainees were released, those of us left behind would ask them to send messages to our families reassuring them that we were okay. We used to lie and say that we were in good health and that things were fine despite the harsh conditions and the illnesses, because we knew that life outside prison was also difficult, amid displacement and starvation.

On June 6, after four and a half months of detention, I was able to meet with my lawyer, Khaled Zabarqa, who reassured me about my family. He told me that, according to my file, there was no charge against me and that I was a prisoner of war.

> "On September 30, I had another court hearing. They told me that there was no charge against me, but the prosecution requested an extension of my detention period for 'helping' or being 'affiliated with' Hamas. They considered any [public sector] employee to be a member of Hamas, so by virtue of my work in the hospital, they considered me to be a member of a terrorist organisation."

He explained that he would be with me in the next court hearing and would try to secure my release. Zabarqa's next visit wasn't until September 17. Throughout the duration of my detention, I was only allowed these two visits with him. He submitted a request for medical treatment when he saw that my health was poor. They told him that they would treat me, but they didn't.

On September 30, I had another court hearing. They told me that there was no charge against me, but the prosecution requested an extension of my detention period for "helping" or being "affiliated with" Hamas. They considered any [public sector] employee to be a member of Hamas, so by virtue of my work in the hospital, they considered me to be a member of a terrorist organisation.

After the Israeli authorities extended my administrative detention again, my lawyer appealed the decision to the Supreme Court. Three months later, on December 31, I had another court hearing and was transferred to Sde Teiman detention centre. There, I was placed in solitary confinement but received health treatment for the first time.

Can you tell us about the moment of your release?

On the 10th day of my treatment, January 10, 2025, they removed my handcuffs and blindfolds early in the morning and transferred me to the Karem Abu Salem [Kerem Shalom] Crossing. There were Red Cross cars there and they told me to go to them. It was an indescribable feeling — I couldn't walk from the emotion. I cried a lot because I finally breathed freedom. For the first time, I saw the sky without bars.

I moved quickly toward the Red Cross vehicle, which took me to Gaza's European Hospital. I was very tired and they asked me to do some medical tests, but I refused and went home. The only thing on my mind was getting home and seeing my family after spending a year in prison.

The hours following my release were hours of joy mixed with pain. I was happy that my family was fine, but saddened by the destruction I saw and the number of relatives and loved ones who were martyred. And I wished that all the prisoners were with me that day to taste freedom.

... /

> "We don't know what the future holds ... It is difficult to think what awaits Gaza."

The day after my release, I went back to the hospital to undergo the rest of the medical tests. They gave me IVs because I was anemic and was suffering from protein deficiency and swelling in my limbs. But I didn't agree to stay in the hospital because my sisters are doctors and I had the opportunity to complete the treatment at home.

Now I am better physically and psychologically, but I still long for the release of the rest of the Palestinian prisoners. I know what it means to be in prison, subjected to torture and humiliation.

How has the gradual return to life in Gaza been?

I couldn't bear not serving patients, so [after some time at home] I returned to Nasser Medical Complex. It was a difficult moment; I got goosebumps. I saw the places I had spent so much time in and remembered the moment of my arrest and the torture I experienced there.

I was very happy that the complex was functioning again — not at its previous capacity, of course. I hope that we will return to serving our people, the sick and wounded, at full capacity — even better than before.

How do you feel about the future?

We don't know what the future holds. The extent of the destruction, the life in tents, the rain and cold weather, the high prices, and the lack of water, services, and many other basic supplies makes it difficult to think about what awaits Gaza. We hope that things improve and we can continue with our daily lives.

•

https://www.972mag.com/abu-shahada-doctor-israeli-detention-abuse/

By imposing a maze of checkpoints, Israel is replicating West Bank conditions in Gaza

26 February 2025
SOURCE: MIDDLE EAST EYE (MEE)

> The world classifies Gaza as north and south, but we, the people of Gaza, know our geography. The one place all of its Palestinian inhabitants love is Gaza City ... For 15 months I have waited to return.

When the Israeli army invaded the Gaza Strip by land and occupied the Netzarim Corridor, which separates the north and south of Gaza, we lived in a state of deep anxiety and fear. How would we return to those areas? Before the war, it was easy for us to go to Gaza City. The world classifies Gaza as north and south, but we, the people of Gaza, know our geography. The one place all of its Palestinian inhabitants love is Gaza City — the centre of business, shopping, and tourism. Indeed, that is, in part, why I missed it so much. For 15 months, I have waited to return.

A long-awaited journey

I live in Khan Yunis, in the south of the Gaza Strip, but my work as a teacher is in Gaza City, which is classified as part of the northern area. I used to go there daily, and the journey took only 20 minutes.

The withdrawal of the Israeli army from the Netzarim Corridor was a dream for all of us — not only for the displaced who longed to return but for everyone in Gaza — because life cannot continue without access to Gaza City and the north. I always promised myself that I would go back the moment the army withdrew.

The long walk home to northern Gaza

My father would ask: "Will you go to report from Gaza and the northern areas when the army withdraws?" My answer was always, "yes". He wanted to come with me to see the beautiful city where we once relaxed in beach cafés. When the Israeli army withdrew at the end of January, we waited for its complete departure. As a resident of the south, I knew I could not stay in the north and would need to return home.

... /

> I also wanted to check on my school, the Rosary Sisters School in Tal al-Hawa. I had taught there for five years, commuting daily without issue. I missed my science lab. I wanted to know it's fate ...

By early February, I checked with friends about the road conditions and checkpoints. Was it crowded? How long would the journey take? Some suggested going by sea, where there was no barrier — only a short walk, after which I could take an animal-drawn cart to reach the Gaza Corniche. It would be quick, they said. But I hesitated. I still had a back injury and severe bruises, and walking would worsen my condition. I decided to wait.

The following Sunday, I had work in Gaza City — I needed to prepare a video story about a girl who had returned north with her family. I also wanted to check on my school, the Rosary Sisters School in Tal al-Hawa. I had taught there for five years, commuting daily without issue. I missed my science lab, where I spent so much time during school hours. I wanted to know of its fate, hoping it had not been destroyed like so many other places during the 2021 war.

An endless maze

That morning, I told my father we were going to Gaza City. At the taxi area, we asked about the road conditions. Would it be crowded? How long would we wait at the checkpoint? These endless questions were exhausting. Before the war, I would go to Gaza City at any time without a second thought. Now, the Israeli army had imposed a painful reality upon us. But we would overcome it.

We found a taxi driver. "Is Salah al-Din Road crowded?" I asked. "Or is it clear?" He reassured me: "Don't worry, we'll get there as quickly as possible. Come with me." My father and I shared the taxi with a family heading north to visit their daughter, who had never left Gaza City during the war. As we drove along Salah al-Din Road and reached Netzarim, we encountered massive sand barriers blocking the street, forcing us onto bypass roads through the Mughraqa area. I wondered what this was. How will we ever get to the check-point?

I felt like we were in a maze. Our driver followed others, navigating a confusing network of rough, unpaved detours. At one point, we stopped — about 30 cars were lined up in front of us, waiting. I stepped out to observe the area. The checkpoint was in a well-lit spot ahead. Around us, deep craters, some as deep as nine metres, scarred the landscape.

> **The checkpoint was in a well-lit spot ahead. Around us, deep craters, some as deep as nine metres, scarred the landscape. The entire Maghraqa area, once a thriving agricultural zone, was now a wasteland.**

The entire Maghraqa area, once a thriving agricultural zone, was now a wasteland. The houses were gone. I checked my watch. I had work to do, and I wanted to visit my school for the first time in 16 months.

A woman in the taxi sighed, "We endured the Israeli army for a year and a half. How do people in the West Bank live like this every day? Their suffering must be immense." Others in the car discussed how the army, unfamiliar with coastal areas like Gaza, had reshaped the land into high sand barriers, mimicking the mountainous terrain of the West Bank.

Unrecognisable roads

As the cars inched forward, I noticed Qatari, American, and Egyptian personnel managing the checkpoint. An Egyptian officer greeted us and asked young men to exit the cars and walk a separate path. My father, at 55 years old, was allowed to stay. We stepped forward and were met by another Egyptian officer, who handed us oranges and water. A Qatari man nearby gave hard-boiled eggs to some children.

Across the way, American soldiers stood in watchtowers, weapons aimed at the road. Sand barriers surrounded them. For the first time in my life, I encountered a checkpoint that actively prevented me from reaching my own city. As we moved past it, I felt relief that I was finally close to Gaza City. But that relief was crushed when I saw the devastation in the Zeitoun neighbourhood, just before the city's entrance. I used to know these roads well. Now, they were unrecognisable. We tried to identify landmarks from what little remained of their walls.

Finally, we reached the area where my school once stood. I asked the driver to stop so I could walk the last stretch. From a distance, I saw the school building — but the outer wall had been destroyed and Israeli bulldozers had razed the yard. As I approached, I took in the destruction: shell damage in the kindergarten and classrooms buried in sand. Guards stood at the internal door. "I'm a teacher here," I told them. "I want to see what happened to the school." Inside, shattered glass littered the floor. Rooms were burned. I hurried to my science lab.

… /

> I checked the condition of the city's main streets … The destruction was widespread. The army had not spared a single area. Universities, hospitals — everything had been reduced to ruins.

Exhausted but hopeful

I went down the stairs and found the lab covered in missile smoke and dust. The windows were shattered, and many of my lab tools were missing. But I was relieved — it had fared better than the library which was completely burned. The classrooms were intact but the schoolyard and theatre, once filled with students' laughter, were destroyed.

The destruction was widespread. The army had not spared a single area. I wanted to clean my lab myself. I tried to open the door, but they told me to wait until next time. Everything around the school had changed. Nothing looked as we remembered. Once again, we were being forced to accept a new reality that Israel had imposed on us.

I could not stay at the school for long — I had to return south. The trip to Gaza City had taken two and a half hours, and I feared being delayed on the way back.

After finishing my work, I checked the condition of the city's main streets, al-Rimal and Unknown Soldier Street. The destruction was widespread. The army had not spared a single area. Universities, hospitals — everything had been reduced to ruins.

At al-Rimal Street, I bought supplies that were unavailable in the south, then told my father it was time to leave. We searched for 30 minutes before finding a car heading south. The journey back was gruelling. The roads were rough and congested, and displaced people were going home. For the first time, I felt the full weight of the distance. The exhaustion was visible on everyone's faces. Gaza is wounded. But it is trying to rise again. Gaza City calls me back, and I hope that one day, the road will be open and free — without a checkpoint.

•

https://www.middleeasteye.net/opinion/maze-checkpoints-israel-replicating-west-bank-conditions-gaza

"We want to live": Rage at Israel fuses with ire at Hamas as protests rock Gaza

27 March 2025
SOURCE: +972 MAGAZINE

> "We've been living under siege for 20 years. There's no work and no future for our youth. Our children are growing up and we don't know what awaits them. How many children have been killed during this war? Are we giving birth to our children only for missiles to kill them in the most horrific way?"

For the past two days, Palestinians across the Gaza Strip have taken to the streets to demand an end to Israel's genocidal onslaught and to Hamas' rule of the territory. Beginning in the northern city of Beit Lahiya, demonstrations quickly spread to other parts of the enclave including Shuja'iyya in the north, Nuseirat and Deir Al-Balah in the centre and Khan Yunis in the south. The protests are the largest since the war began, and the most significant public display of dissent against Hamas in Gaza in years.

The demonstrations were triggered by new Israeli orders to evacuate Beit Lahiya and the surrounding areas, as the military expands its latest ground incursion. Residents spontaneously went out onto the streets on Tuesday to vent their anger at being forcibly displaced yet again, reflecting the population's increasing desperation after Israel shattered the fragile ceasefire last week.

While holding Israel responsible for the slaughter of more than 50,000 people over the past year and a half, and for subjecting the Strip to a longstanding blockade that has further intensified during the war, the protesters are also directing their ire at Hamas: they are calling on the group to do everything in its power to stop the bombing before stepping aside to allow for free elections.

"I participated in the demonstrations from the moment they started," 50-year-old Raed Tabash, from Khan Yunis, told +972. "I chanted and screamed and vented my inner rage. We've been living under siege for 20 years. There's no work and no future for our youth. Our children are growing up and we don't know what awaits them. How many children have been killed during this war? Are we giving birth to our children only for missiles to kill them in the most horrific way?

… /

> "Hamas is part of Gaza; some of us agree with it and some disagree with it — this is normal. We are calling for elections, to change who rules us. This is our right as a people who want to change our reality and our future …"

"I'm tired of being repeatedly displaced," Tabash continued. "I have no money left to buy food for my children, and even if I did, the markets are empty. We have become physically and psychologically ill. We want a complete and final end to the war, and for elections to be held so we can choose a party other than Hamas to govern us. I will not stop going out and demanding an end to our suffering until all of this stops and there is a change in the government in Gaza."

Despite his criticisms of Hamas, however, Tabash emphasised that his main struggle is against the Israeli occupation. "If we were freed from the shackles of the occupier and from its repeated wars, we and our children would live in safety and peace," he stated. "The occupation is responsible for our suffering."

Ahmed Thabet, 29, participated in protests this week in Beit Lahiya. "As a young man, I have a future: I want to work, get married, and have a family," he told +972. "A year and a half have passed since the war started and there has been no change in the reality that the occupation has imposed on us. There is only a daily routine of killing, destruction, and crying over our loved ones. If the missiles don't kill us, famine will. We want to change this reality.

"The world thinks that all of Gaza is Hamas, which is false," Thabet continued. "Hamas is part of Gaza; some of us agree with it and some disagree with it — this is normal. We are calling for elections, to change who rules us. This is our right as a people who want to change our reality and our future. The war must stop, and Hamas' rule must be replaced.

"Keep in mind that in the West Bank, which is ruled by the Palestinian Authority, Palestinians suffer from displacement, arrests, and home demolitions [by the Israeli military]," he went on. "This means that the occupation is against the Palestinian people, not against their political affiliation. I hope the United States will support us in our right to live and stop supporting and perpetuating the war. We will help the negotiators to successfully reach a solution to end it."

Munir Baraka, a 45-year-old from Deir Al-Balah, hit back at the cynical support for the protests from the Israeli media and politicians. "We don't care what they say, nor that they are

> **Munir Baraka, a 45-year-old from Deir Al-Balah, hit back at the cynical support for the protests from the Israeli media and politicians … "We don't care what they say … We want a responsible body that cares about our lives and our future. No party has the right to force us to live through successive and continuous wars."**

encouraging us to demonstrate. We are against the occupation and their war. We are calling for a change in Hamas' rule, as is our right — just as the Israelis are calling for the overthrow of Netanyahu's government."

"Hamas has ruled Gaza since 2007, and it is time for its role to end," he continued. "We don't want the Palestinian Authority either, because we see what it has done in the West Bank. We want a responsible body that cares about our lives and our future. No party has the right to force us to live through successive and continuous wars. We want the world to see Gazans as human beings like them — a free, peaceful, civil people who want to live." Baraka went on: "None of us wants death. Whoever calls us terrorists to justify the occupation killing us with heavy missiles is wrong. We support any negotiations to stop the war, and we will continue these demonstrations until our demands are met."

"It's clear the sound of our empty stomachs bothered you"

Beyond the protests on Gaza's streets, Palestinians also took to social media to defend the demonstrators against accusations that they were doing the bidding of Israel or the Palestinian Authority.

"Those who took part in the spontaneous demonstrations in northern Gaza are the same people who starved, surviving on animal fodder and wild grass," Sami Abu Salem wrote in a post on Facebook. "They are the ones who endured and foiled [Israel's] displacement plan. They are the ones still waiting for their children to be pulled from the rubble. They are the ones whose names belong on the honour roll. I believe their protest was spontaneous and has nothing to do with the Palestinian Authority or anyone else," he continued. "Accusing them of treason is shamelessness and moral and political bankruptcy."

Others directly addressed those opposing the protests. "Dear ones who have the right to speak about us … We apologise for the unexpected surprise, as we are people of flesh and blood like you," Ahmed Mortaja wrote on Facebook. "We tried to fast without complaining about the lack of food and drink for more than 18 months, but it is clear that the sound of our empty stomachs bothered you. We apologise for that."

… /

> "Israel does not want disarmament, but rather the annihilation of existence. If Hamas surrenders its weapons without a real guarantee of a path toward liberation and statehood, Israel will transform the Strip into a darker version of Sabra and Shatila."

Some, like Saleh Fayaz, expressed anger and frustration with Hamas while acknowledging that in the current circumstances it is the only thing preventing Gaza's total eradication. "I have enough criticism of Hamas to write a book of five hundred pages or more," he wrote. "But since October 7, Hamas has not been the target. It has only been the pretext."

"Had Hamas been completely annihilated, Israel would have continued its war against the Mujahideen Brigades and the Popular Front, turning every raised rifle into an 'imminent danger,'" he continued. "Israel does not want disarmament, but rather the annihilation of existence. If Hamas surrenders its weapons without a real guarantee of a path toward liberation and statehood, Israel will transform the Strip into a darker version of Sabra and Shatila."

Fayaz also responded to social media posts by pro-Israel influencers expressing support for the protests and urging Gazans to join them. "Calls by Zionists like Edy Cohen to demonstrate are likely an attempt to hijack the movement and undermine the protesters," he said. "Those who might have joined the protests would [instead] hold back so as not to be seen as following Israeli orders."

"I believe Israel wants to preserve the image it has projected to the world, that all of Gaza is of one colour and deserving of death because [its people supposedly] support 'terrorism,'" he added. "What it doesn't want to show is the real picture emerging — that Gaza is in fact multi-coloured."

•

https://www.972mag.com/gaza-protests-war-israel-hamas/

"I am not a number, I am a real story from Gaza. Remember it."

6 April 2025
SOURCE: AL JAZEERA

I am the girl who studied for high school and university under exceptional circumstances when Gaza was under a very tight siege. I completed university and looked for work everywhere to help my father, who was exhausted by the siege and had lost his job ...

I've been thinking about writing a will. I didn't expect to feel death so close to me. I used to say death comes suddenly, we don't feel it, but during this war, they made us feel everything ... slowly.

We suffer before it happens, like expecting your house to be bombed. It may still be standing since the start of the war, but that feeling of fear remains within you. This fear has worn my heart down, till I feel like it can't handle anything more.

Since the beginning of the war, I've been struggling with the Israeli army being so close to us. I remember the moment tanks entered from the Netzarim area, and I sent a message to all my friends, shocked: "How did they enter Gaza? Am I dreaming?!"

I was waiting for them to withdraw from Gaza, for it to be free again, like we had always known it. Now they're so close to where I am, in al-Fukhari, east of Khan Yunis and north of Rafah. It's the point where Khan Yunis ends and Rafah begins.

They're so close, forcing us to hear terrifying explosions every moment, making us endure those endless sounds. This war is different, so different from what I've experienced before.

That has been stuck in my head since I saw martyrs being referred to as "unknown persons" or placed in mass graves. Some of them are even body parts that couldn't be identified. Is it possible that all it would say on my shroud would be "a young woman in a black/blue blouse"? Could I die as an "unknown person", just a number? I want everyone around me to remember my story. I am not a number.

I am the girl who studied for high school and university under exceptional circumstances when Gaza was under a very tight siege. I completed university and looked for work everywhere to help my father, who was exhausted by the siege and had lost his job several times.

... /

> **I am the eldest daughter in my family ... I don't want to forget anything.
> I am a refugee. My grandparents were refugees who were forced by the Israeli occupation to leave our occupied land in 1948.**

I am the eldest daughter in my family, and I wanted to help my father and for us to have a good home to live in. Wait ... I don't want to forget anything. I am a refugee. My grandparents were refugees who were forced by the Israeli occupation to leave our occupied land in 1948. They moved to the Gaza Strip and lived in the Khan Yunis refugee camp, west of the city.

I was born in that camp, but the Israeli army didn't let me continue my life there. They demolished our house in 2000, and we were left without shelter for two years. We moved from one uninhabitable house to another, until UNRWA gave us another house in 2003 in al-Fukhari. That wonderful area, with all the farmland, where we tried to build a life in the neighbourhood, that was named "European Housing", after the European Hospital located there.

The house was small, not enough for a family of five, with a father and a mother. It needed extra rooms, a living room, and the kitchen needed work. We lived there for about 12 years anyway, and as soon as I could, I started working in 2015 to help my father. I helped him make the house comfortable to live in. Yes, we achieved that, but it was so hard. We finished building our home just three months before October 7, 2023.

Yes, nearly 10 years I spent rebuilding it piece by piece according to our financial ability, and we just managed to finish it right before the war. When the war came, I was already exhausted, from the siege and the difficulty of life in Gaza. Then the war came to completely drain me, wear down my heart and make me lose my focus.

I wake up running

We've been fighting for something since the beginning of the war. Fighting for survival, fighting not to die from hunger or thirst, fighting not to lose our minds from the horrors we witness and experience. We try to survive by any means. We've gone through the displacement — in my life I've lived in four houses, and every one ended up near bombardment by the Israeli army. We don't have a safe place to be. Before the ceasefire, we lived 500 days of sheer terror.

What I didn't do during the war, unfortunately, was cry. I tried to stay strong and kept my sadness and anger inside, which exhausted

I am not a number, I am a real story from Gaza. Remember it.

> **I haven't really slept in over a week. I doze off, I'm woken by the sounds of explosions and wake up running. I don't know where I'm trying to go, but I run through the house.**

my heart and weakened it even more. I was positive and supportive of everyone around me. Yes, the people from the north will return. Yes, the army will withdraw from Netzarim. I wanted to give everyone strength, while inside me there was great weakness I didn't want to show. I felt that if it showed, I would perish in this terrifying war.

The ceasefire was my great hope for survival. I felt like I had made it. The war was over. When people wondered: "Will the war return?" I confidently replied, "No, I don't think it will. The war is over."

The war did return, and closer than ever to me. I lived the continuous fear brought on by never-ending shelling. They used every kind of weapon against us — rockets, shells from planes and tanks. The tanks kept firing, surveillance drones kept flying; everything was terrifying.

I haven't really slept for over a week. If I doze off, I'm woken up by the sound of explosions and wake up running. I don't know where I am trying to go, but I run through the house.

In the constant panic, I put my hand on my heart, wondering if it would withstand much more. That's why I sent a message to all my friends, asking them to talk about my story so that I would not just be a number.

We are living through unbearable days as the Israeli army destroys the neighbourhood around me. Many families are still living here. They don't want to leave because displacement is exhausting — physically, financially, and mentally.

The first displacement I remember was the one in 2000, when I was about eight years old. Israeli army bulldozers came into the Khan Yunis camp and destroyed my uncle's house and my grandfather's. Then, for some reason, they stopped at our house. So, we left. It was Ramadan and my parents figured we could come back later. They found a dilapidated shell of a house for us to shelter in, temporarily, they thought.

I couldn't bear the idea that we had lost our home, so I would run back to the house where all those beautiful memories with my grandparents were, and I would grab a few things to take back to my mother.

... /

I am not a number, I am a real story from Gaza. Remember it.

> **I don't know what the future holds if the world doesn't save us from this terrifying army. I don't know if my heart will withstand these endless sounds any more. Don't ever forget me.**

The Israeli army demolished our house the night before Eid, and my family and I went there on the first day of Eid al-Fitr. I clearly remember celebrating Eid on the rubble, wearing my new Eid outfit.

The Israeli army doesn't let us keep anything; it destroys everything, leaving us with nothing but sorrow in our hearts. I don't know what the future holds if the world doesn't save us from this terrifying army. I don't know if my heart will withstand these endless sounds any more. Don't ever forget me.

I've fought hard for my life. I've worked hard, as a journalist and a teacher for 10 years, dedicating myself. I have students I love and colleagues with whom I have beautiful memories. Life in Gaza has never been easy, but we love it, and we can't love any other home.

•

https://www.aljazeera.com/features/2025/4/6/i-am-not-a-number-i-am-a-great-story-from-gaza-remember-it

"Rafah became my home after displacement. It is now being erased."

12 April 2025
SOURCE: MIDDLE EAST EYE (MEE)

Before October 2023, Rafah — a city covering nearly one-fifth of the Gaza Strip — was home to 350,000 residents. During the war, it gained international visibility as a supposed safe zone for one million displaced Palestinians.

On Wednesday, *Ha'aretz* reported that Israel is preparing to expand its "buffer zone", swallowing Rafah and its surrounding neighbourhoods in southern Gaza. The city — once the last refuge for displaced Palestinians — has been reduced to rubble after weeks of relentless bombardment. The few residents who remained after earlier evacuations have now been forced to flee once more, this time to a so-called "humanitarian zone" near Khan Yunis and al-Mawasi — a site site marked by starvation, repeated attacks and overwhelming suffering.

Since breaking the ceasefire in March, the Israeli military has continued carving the Gaza Strip into isolated zones as part of its ongoing project of territorial theft and ethnic cleansing.

Before October 2023, Rafah — a city covering nearly one-fifth of the Gaza Strip — was home to 350,000 residents. During the war, it gained international visibility as a supposed safe zone for one million displaced Palestinians. My family and I had also experienced displacement and sought refuge near Rafah after losing our home more than 20 years ago. It was not my childhood home, but it became a place I grew to cherish. Despite viral social media posts urging the world to keep "all eyes on Rafah" — in the belief that international scrutiny might deter Israel from targeting vulnerable families sheltering in tents — the world has chosen to turn a blind eye and leave Rafah to an unknown fate. But the destruction of a place does not erase its memory or the traces of life left behind by those who called it home.

Found refuge

Before we settled in Rafah, I spent the first eight years of my life with my grandparents in a house in the Khan Yunis refugee camp, just west of the city. I considered it my true childhood home.

... /

> **It was on the night of Eid al-Fitr that the army came to demolish our homes, turning what should have been a night of joy into one of devastation. It is a painful memory. I still yearn for that house.**

Unfortunately, we lived next to several Israeli army observation posts. I would open the door and see soldiers patrolling or stationed just metres away, within their fortified positions. We faced many difficulties due to their proximity until they ultimately demolished our house in 2000.

My uncles, grandfather and I all lived in that area. Our homes were close together, and we had wonderful neighbours. It was on the night of Eid al-Fitr that the army came to demolish our homes, turning what should have been a night of joy into one of devastation. It is a painful memory. I still yearn for that house. It holds some of the most beautiful moments from my early years.

After two years of moving from one temporary shelter to another following the destruction of our home, the local authorities eventually gave us a house in al-Fakhari, near Rafah.

This town was mostly agricultural and sparsely populated, with the feel of a quiet village. Over time, the arrival of displaced families like ours brought more life and activity to the area.

We moved into that house in 2002. Not long after, the government began to classify al-Fakhari as part of Rafah, treating it as one of the city's districts. At the time, though, I had never truly been to Rafah — apart from one brief visit in 2003 when I was in middle school.

We were preparing to buy Eid clothes and my mother suggested we go to the Rafah market instead of the one in Khan Yunis. We went after we broke our fasts, around 6pm (3pm GMT). Though it was only a short visit, seeing Rafah for the first time left a lasting impression. It was bustling with people, full of life and shops. There was a well-known area in downtown Rafah called al-Awda roundabout, but we did not venture too deeply into it because we were not familiar with the city. I remember my mother getting very tired from all the walking and she sat near al-Awda Mosque — a large and beautiful mosque, one of Rafah's main landmarks.

We eventually returned home, but the memory of that day has stayed with me, becoming more vivid every time Rafah is mentioned.

Rafah became my home after displacement. It is now being erased.

> Many wars have befallen Gaza, and Rafah has remained resilient through them all — including the 2014 war, which claimed many lives in the city.

Deepening ties

Many wars have befallen Gaza, including the 2014 war, which claimed many lives in the city, and Rafah has remained resilient through them all. The situation became so dire that the health ministry was forced to place bodies in ice cream freezers due to a lack of space in morgues.

After successive wars in the Gaza Strip, Rafah residents began calling on the world to support the construction of a hospital, as it was the only city in Gaza without one. We all spoke up, repeating Rafah's name again and again, trying to amplify that demand. My work in journalism led me to move between cities, and Rafah became part of that routine — mainly because of how close it was.

Government authorities eventually reclassified al-Fakhari as part of the city of Khan Yunis. But our physical and emotional proximity to Rafah kept it close to our hearts. I would visit occasionally when I had stories to film or to write about, but I did not go regularly. I did not know much about Rafah's neighbourhoods until I was offered an unexpected opportunity that brought me there every week.

In 2020, an NGO suggested I lead educational science activities for children in a remote part of Rafah. These sessions were to support their schoolwork and give them a chance to learn in a more engaging environment. I hesitated at first. I already worked full-time as a teacher and only had Sundays off. But I love supporting students in whatever way I can, so I gave up my day and began travelling weekly to Tal al-Sultan, an area west of Rafah. That neighbourhood is now completely destroyed; its landmarks are erased.

But over those months, my connection to Rafah deepened. I developed small rituals. I remembered my mother sitting to rest near al-Awda Mosque 17 years earlier. She is now ill and has struggled for years with spinal problems. I began donating to the mosque each week, asking God to accept this small offering and heal her. Every visit began the same way: I would stop at the donation box before continuing to Tal al-Sultan. Rafah welcomed me each week. The children at the centre would wait at the door to greet me with joy. I tried to bring them happiness through recreational activities, and they returned it tenfold with their warmth, eagerness and gratitude.

... /

Rafah became my home after displacement. It is now being erased.

> For over a year we relied on Rafah. But when the army began its operations there, our area became trapped between two front lines, and life grew increasingly difficult. I hear and feel every missile that strikes the city.

Shattered refuge

From October 2023 to May 2024, Rafah hosted more than a million displaced people. The army falsely promoted it to the world as a "safe" and "humanitarian" zone. It received aid and opened its doors to everyone.

When the ground invasion began in Khan Yunis in December 2023, we could no longer reach the city for even the most basic supplies. For over a year, we relied on Rafah. But when the army began its operations there, our area became trapped between two front lines, and life grew increasingly difficult. I hear and feel every missile that strikes the city. We see the smoke rise to the sky. The destruction is relentless — without red lines, without pause.

For a week now, the army has been bulldozing, demolishing and levelling the Mirage area next to us. It is the northern gateway to Rafah, an agricultural zone and a vital source of food for the south. It helped feed Gaza during the repeated closures of the crossings. Now, we hear constant shelling. Heavy missiles fall as if they were throwing stones — without mercy. Many families are still trapped in northern Rafah. They have chosen to die in their homes rather than flee again.

Displacement has been a bitter, exhausting experience for everyone, which is why so many refuse to leave. We, too, have stayed. We do not want to flee. Each night, we pray that we will survive another day. The sounds of bombing are terrifying, but even worse are the moments when warplanes open fire on the areas around us.

Rafah — and every part of Gaza — is a land of freedom because its people seek to live in peace and dignity, free on their land, without wars or occupation.

We are struggling to survive here. Rafah is barely breathing beneath the bombs, bulldozers and destruction. It has not remained on its land, but Rafah will remain in the hearts of those who knew it as the fortress of steadfastness that the people of Gaza have always known.

•

https://www.middleeasteye.net/opinion/rafah-became-home-after-displacement-now-being-erased

Rafah became my home after displacement. It is now being erased.

A ruined university in northern Gaza becomes a refuge.

15 April 2025
SOURCE: +972 MAGAZINE

"I didn't even consider sheltering in UNRWA schools because the army always targets them," Omar Al-Za'anin explained, sensing that the university was their safest option.

In the early morning hours of March 22, Omar Al-Za'anin, 60, and his family of six hurriedly left their home under heavy rainfall in the northern Gaza neighbourhood of Beit Hanoun. Five nights earlier, as Israel unleashed a wave of deadly strikes across the enclave — killing 400 people and injuring hundreds — the army dropped evacuation leaflets over Al-Za'anin's neighborhood, declaring it a "combat zone" and urging them to evacuate immediately to known shelters in western Gaza City.

While many left northern Gaza for Khan Yunis, hundreds of families sought refuge in the Islamic University west of Gaza City, which has remained severely damaged since Israel bombed the campus just days after October 7. Al-Za'anin's family was one of them. "I didn't even consider [sheltering in] UNRWA schools because the army always targets them," he explained, sensing that the university was their safest option.

After multiple displacements, Al-Za'anin's family had just begun to feel safe again during the latest ceasefire, when they returned to Beit Hanoun. "We wanted to cultivate our agricultural lands and rebuild our lives and the lives of our children — we felt the suffering was over," he told +972. Now, he continued, "we are still in a state of deep shock from the return of the war," as Israel pummels Gaza with a newfound intensity.

Each day begins with thinking about how to secure water and make bread. "We live on aid; we have no income at all. Every-thing is expensive, at double the price," Al-Za'anin explained. Despite being ordered by the Israeli army to evacuate west, the university doesn't feel much safer than Beit Hanoun. "The bombing continues around us, and we expect death at any moment — I ask the world to look at us with humanity, to end the war, and to give us a chance to live with our children."

... /

> For Suham Naseer, a 50-year-old mother of eight, the Islamic University is the eighth place to which she and her family have been displaced since Israel's onslaught began in October 2023.

The shelter is also a perverse reminder to the displaced that Gaza's youth have been deprived of anything resembling a proper education for a year and a half. "Universities are a place to educate our children, not a refuge for the displaced," Al-Za'anin said. By January of last year, all of Gaza's schools had been shut, including all 12 of its universities which were at various times the target of Israeli attacks. The 90,000 university students in Gaza enrolled before the war have been largely unable to continue their studies for the second year in a row, with thousands of other students and faculty likely killed.

For Suham Naseer, a 50-year-old mother of eight, the Islamic University is the eighth place to which she and her family have been displaced since Israel's onslaught began in October 2023. Desperate for fuel, Naseer explained that those sheltering in the university have been forced to collect and burn the scattered academic books in order to heat food, boil water, and stay warm.

Like Al-Za'anin, Naseer and her family had returned to Beit Hanoun after the ceasefire. "We thought the war was over and we had escaped death, but suddenly the war and heavy bombing returned," she said. The never-ending displacements have become harder and harder for her family to bear: "At least the martyrs have been relieved of this suffering," Naseer remarked.

Subhi Al-Kharawat, 35, from Beit Hanoun took refuge in the university for the sake of his ill wife and newborn child, after spending the war's first 16 months seeking shelter in southern Gaza. "If I did not have a family, I never would have evacuated to the south at the beginning of the war — it was an attempt to save my children from death," he told +972.

In mid-February, while the ceasefire was still in effect, Al-Kharawat's wife gave birth on their long journey from southern Gaza to the north. She has not had a chance to properly recover from the birth and the exhausting trek — even inside the university walls. "Everyone around me is busy setting up tents here and providing water and food. Our days are occupied with searching for basic necessities of life," he said. At night, the shelling doesn't stop. "We want the world to stop this. Enough war. We are so tired of all this," Al-Kharawat lamented.

> **And as Israel continues to prevent all humanitarian aid from entering Gaza — now for over six weeks — even obtaining water is like discovering treasure.**

Khalil Issa Naseer, 52, from Beit Hanoun arrived at the Islamic University with nothing but a tent after being forcibly displaced from his home on March 18 when Israel shattered the ceasefire. When the army ordered Naseer and his three children to move to western Gaza City from Beit Hanoun, they knew the drill. "The occupation forces give us a short period of time to leave and then begin attacking us with artillery shells and aircrafts," he explained.

The university building is crowded, and it has been difficult for Naseer and his family to get settled. "We are looking for a square meter of land, either an area to pitch a tent or a grave to be buried in," he told +972. And as Israel continues to prevent all humanitarian aid from entering Gaza — now for over six weeks — even obtaining water is like discovering treasure, Naseer said. "The occupation has cut off our water, electricity and food."

Despite finding shelter for the time being, Naseer knows that any sense of security is merely temporary. "We never feel safe in Gaza," he said. "The Islamic University which graduated countless doctors, engineers and professors has already basically been reduced to rubble. Now what will happen to it?"

•

https://www.972mag.com/islamic-university-refuge-northern-gaza/

In Gaza the Nakba is being relived in 2025

15 May 2025
SOURCE: AL JALZEERA

> **I was born a refugee in the Khan Yunis camp, known by the city's residents as the largest gathering of refugees expelled from their lands during the Nakba, when Israel was founded in 1948.**

The Nakba. It's a concept that accompanied me from birth until I lived through it myself these past two years. I was born a refugee in the Khan Yunis camp, known by the city's residents as the largest gathering of refugees expelled from their lands during the Nakba, when Israel was founded in 1948.

Whenever someone asked me my name, it was always followed by: "Are you a refugee or a citizen?"

What is a refugee?

As a child, I would ask: "What is a refugee?" I attended a school run by UNRWA, the United Nations Relief and Works Agency for Palestine Refugees, and my documents always had to include proof that I was a refugee.

I received treatment at UNRWA clinics, always needing to bring that refugee card. I spent a lot of time trying to understand what being a refugee meant. How did my grandparents flee their land in Beit Daras, a village north of the Gaza Strip that no longer exists? How did my grandfather end up in this camp, and why did he choose this place?

Before Israel's war on Gaza, May 15, or Nakba Day, the day Palestinians commemorate the Nakba, was a unique occasion. Everyone paid attention to it, seeking out people who had lived through it to hear their stories.

When I began working as a journalist in 2015, Nakba Day was one of the events I looked forward to covering. That year, I went along with colleagues to the Shati camp, west of Gaza City. It would be my first time writing about the Nakba, and my first visit to a refugee camp in 13 years, since we had moved from camp life to village life in al-Fukhari, south of Khan Yunis.

… /

> **We sat with elderly women, all over 70. They talked about their homeland, the stability they had in their lands, their simple lives, the food they grew and ate, and the heartbreak of not being able to return.**

When I entered the camp, memories of my childhood in Khan Yunis came flooding back: the small, crowded houses, some newly built, others still original structures.

It was nice that the commemoration falls in May, with good weather. Elderly men and women sat by their doors, just as my grandmother did when I was a child. I used to love sitting with her; she seemed used to open spaces, like her pre-1948 home in Beit Daras.

We sat with elderly women, all over 70. They talked about their homeland, the stability they had in their lands, their simple lives, the food they grew and ate, and the heartbreak of not being able to return.

We met many people — from Majdal, Hamama, and al-Jura, all depopulated villages and towns taken over by Israel in 1948. Whenever I met someone from Beit Daras, we'd share memories, and laugh a lot, talking about the maftoul (Palestinian couscous) the town was famous for. The visit was light-hearted, filled with laughter and nostalgia, despite these people having been forced into camp life after the occupation drove them from their towns in horrific ways.

Displacement

I had began to understand those Nakba stories more deeply when my grandfather told me his own story. He became the central character in my Nakba reports every year, until his death in 2021.

He estimated he was about 15 years old at the time. He was already married to my grandmother, and they had a child. He would describe the scenes as I sat in awe, asking myself: How could the world have stood by silently?

My grandfather told me they had a good life, working their farm, eating from their crops. Each town had a specialty, and they exchanged produce. Theirs was a simple cuisine, with lots of lentils and bread made from wheat they ground in stone mills. Until that dreadful displacement. He said the Zionist militias forced them to leave, ordering them to go to nearby Gaza.

> **After hours of walking they reached Khan Yunis and, with nowhere else to go, he pitched a tent. Eventually UNRWA was set up and gave him a home, the one I remember from childhood.**

My grandfather said he shut the door to his home, took my grandmother and their son — just a few months old — and started walking. Israeli planes hovered overhead, firing at people as if to drive them to move faster.

The baby — my uncle — didn't survive the journey. My grandfather never wanted to go into the details, he would only say that their son died from the conditions as they fled.

After hours of walking, they reached Khan Yunis and, with nowhere else to go, he pitched a tent. Eventually, UNRWA was set up and gave him a home, the one I remember from my childhood. It was so old; I spent years visiting them in that asbestos-roofed house with its aged walls.

That memory of being forced into exile became their wound. Yet, the idea of return, the right to go home, was sustained through successive generations.

Memories made flesh, blood, and anguish

The Nakba was a memory passed down from the elderly to the young. But in the war that Israel began waging on Gaza on October 7, 2023, we lived the Nakba again. We were forcibly displaced under threat of weapons and air strikes. We saw our loved ones arrested before our eyes and tortured in prisons. We lived in tents and searched everywhere for basic provisions to save our children.

My grandfather told me they fled under threat of weapons and planes — so did we. He said they searched for flour, food, and water while trying to protect their children — so are we, right now in the 21st century.

Perhaps in 1948, the media was more primitive. But now, the world watches what's happening in Gaza in many formats — written, visual, and audio — and yet, nothing has changed. Never did I imagine I'd live through an existential war — a war that threatens my very presence on my land, just as my grandparents lived through. The repeated scenes of displacement are so painful. They're a cycle, one that we have been cursed to live through as Palestinians again and again.

… /

> We will tell
> future generations
> about this war,
> the war of existence.
> We resist hunger,
> fear, thirst, and pain
> so we can remain
> on this land.

Will history record this as Nakba 2025?

Years from now, will we speak of this Nakba just as we've spoken about the original one for 77 years? Will we tell stories, hold commemorations, and hold close memories of the dream of return that has stayed with us since childhood?

Since I realised what it meant to be called a refugee and learned I had a homeland, I've been dreaming of returning. This pain, we can never forget it. I still remember the camp and my life there.

I'll never forget the moment Israel destroyed my house and made us homeless for two years, 24 years ago. Now we live our painful days searching for safety, fighting to survive.

We will tell future generations about this war, the war of existence. We resist hunger, fear, thirst, and pain so we can remain on this land. The Nakba hasn't ended. The 1948 Nakba continues in 2025.

•

https://www.aljazeera.com/features/2025/5/15/gaza-nakba-relived-2025

Gaza's Al-Baqa Cafe was a sanctuary amid the genocide. Now it lies in ruins.

3 July 2025
SOURCE: +972 MAGAZINE

The Israeli army dropped a 500-pound bomb on the cafe without any warning. According to Gaza's Health Ministry, the airstrike killed at least 33 people including the cafe's owner, Saher Al-Baqa.

For over two decades, Al-Baqa Cafe was a cherished seaside refuge in western Gaza City, a place for family and friends to meet or those seeking a quiet space to rest or do some work. The cafe's simple two-level wooden structure, with open balconies shaded by umbrellas, overlooked the Mediterranean Sea, and its owners kept prices low to remain affordable to the community.

Al-Baqa was one of the few businesses in Gaza that managed to stay open despite the war. It provided internet access to students continuing their studies, journalists filing reports, and freelancers trying to work amid frequent power blackouts and repeated displacement. As life across the Strip ground to a halt, people gathered at Al-Baqa on plastic chairs, sipping whatever drinks were still available under the blockade, and stealing brief moments of calm with colleagues and loved ones.

That all came to an end around noon on Monday, June 30, when the Israeli army dropped a 500-pound bomb on the cafe without any warning. According to Gaza's Health Ministry, the airstrike killed at least 33 people including the cafe's owner, Saher Al-Baqa.

After the bombing, the Israeli army claimed it had "attacked a number of terrorists from the Hamas terrorist organisation" and that "prior to the attack, many steps were taken to reduce the chance of harming civilians." A week later, on July 7, the Israeli army and Shin Bet released another statement claiming, without further evidence, that the victims of the strike included the commander of Hamas' naval forces in northern Gaza and two other "terrorists."

Maher Al-Baqa, Saher's brother and co-owner of the cafe, expressed sorrow and disbelief over the bombing. "The public's grief shows that the cafe was simply a place for ordinary people — it had no

... /

> ... the cafe was simply a place for ordinary people — despite what the Israeli army claims ... It was a place for recreation and comfort and a friend to everyone.

other purpose, despite what the [Israeli army] claims," he told +972 Magazine. "It was a place for recreation and comfort and a friend to everyone since the beginning of the war. I am still in deep shock that it was targeted."

"We mourn everything there, even the walls"

Ismail Abu Hatab, a 32-year-old photojournalist from Gaza City, was among those killed in the strike. A regular at the cafe for years, he often came to meet with friends and colleagues, trying to maintain a routine throughout the war.

Abu Hatab was known for capturing Gaza's natural beauty. But the war forced him to document the death and displacement unfolding along the coast — scenes later featured in his photography exhibition "Between the Sky and the Sea," which was displayed in several U.S. states.

In November 2023, Abu Hatab was seriously wounded when an Israeli airstrike targeted the Al-Ghifari Tower in Gaza City, which housed the Palestinian Media Group's offices. Yet he continued to work as a photojournalist, and after returning to Gaza City during the ceasefire in February, he resumed photographing life by the sea, determined to portray Gaza's enduring humanity.

"This is not an ordinary loss, but rather the loss of a dear, creative friend in a place that holds so many memories," Salem Al-Rayes, Abu Hatab's close friend and fellow freelance journalist, told +972.

"I met Ismail several years ago through mutual friends. We got to know each other well and we would meet to talk about work and life. He told me about his reluctance to work as much after being injured at the beginning of the war, which nearly resulted in the amputation of his left leg."

The two had met the previous weekend in a different cafe in the central city of Deir Al-Balah, and had begun running training sessions for a group of journalists. Al-Rayes arrived in Gaza City on Sunday, where he led the next session. "[Abu Hatab] was supposed to complete their training over the next two days, just as we did with the first group last week," he explained.

> In the days since the strike, many Palestinians have written heartfelt tributes to Al-Baqa, describing their deep and enduring affection for the cafe, and mourning the loss of yet another Gazan landmark ...

At the end of the Sunday meeting, one of the journalists-in-training asked Al-Rayes a question he couldn't answer. "I told her to bring it up with Ismail the next day, as he was the most experienced in his field," he told +972. "I didn't know that we would say goodbye to him so soon."

Frans Al-Salmi, a visual artist from Gaza City and a close friend of Abu Hatab, was martyred alongside him in the coffeeshop. "She was very kind and gentle," Nelly Khalid, who had been friends with Al-Salmi for several years, told +972. "We used to go to [Al-Baqa Cafe] together, and we were planning to meet there again once the war is over."

"We mourn everything there, even the walls," Khalid continued. "[Al-Salmi] was an ambitious girl. She worked with Ismail, [helping to] launch the website for their media platform 'ByPa' [where Gazan creators share stories about their lives and identities]. Fate was faster than anything. They departed together and we will meet in heaven."

"This is the only place I loved in Gaza"

In the days since the strike, many Palestinians have written heartfelt tributes to Al-Baqa, describing their deep and enduring affection for the cafe, and mourning the loss of yet another Gazan landmark.

Maryam Al-Akhras, 28, from Gaza City, grew up with the cafe as her happy place. "This is the only place I loved in Gaza," she said. "Since childhood, I went there with my school friends every weekend. They allowed us to bring food from outside if we wanted. Then in high school, whenever I felt stressed from studying, I would go there alone, sitting at a table by the sea. In university, we would go there to celebrate our birthdays and other happy occasions."

During the war, Al-Baqa remained Al-Akhra's escape. "I kept going there to relax [and get] away from the war. However, on the day of the attack, I had been displaced from the Al-Daraj area [of Gaza City] due to the Israeli army's new evacuation orders, so I didn't go to the cafe. I told my family that when we settle in our relatives' house on the beach, Al-Baqa would be closer to us, and I could go every day."

... /

> **Abdallah Karam Seyam of Gaza City reflected on what the cafe meant to him. "Al-Baqa wasn't just a place," he wrote. "It was a small refuge for laughter, for sweet gatherings with my family and friends."**

"When I read the news of the cafe's targeting, I felt a great shock — they chose the thing that makes us happy, and they destroyed it," she continued. "I feel very sad about losing this place and its people. I hope the war ends before we all die."

Yusuf Salah Al-Ashqar, a longtime regular at Al-Baqa Cafe, reflected on the loss in a Facebook post. "It was practically the only outlet, the only place you could go to — whether you had money or not — to sit, enjoy, and order the same things."

"Despite its simplicity, I saw it as more of a cultural space than just a seaside cafe," he added. "In the year when the crossings were more regularly open, I even used it to host guests."

In another post, Abdallah Karam Seyam of Gaza City reflected on what the cafe meant to him. "Al-Baqa wasn't just a place," he wrote. "It was a small refuge for laughter, for sweet gatherings with my family and friends. We tucked away pieces of our lives there, spent long nights, and lived moments that will never come again."

Among those killed in the strike was Naseem Abu Sabha, whose fiancée, Ola, was wounded and hospitalised. In their statement on July 7, the Israeli army and Shin Bet declared, without evidence, that Naseem was a "terrorist." Ola denied this to +972, stating: "The army always lies to justify its bombing and killing of innocent and ordinary people."

In a social media post from her hospital bed at Al-Shifa, Ola recounted her final moments with her fiancée. The couple had been sharing coffee and falafel sandwiches while they discussed travelling together, Naseem's hopes to meet Ola's mother, and his pride in having won her heart.

"He was sitting beside me ... and we took many pictures," Ola said. "He was almost fluttering with joy, telling me how beautiful the photos were ... He held my hand the whole time. Even when we spoke of death, he told me not to worry, as long as we were together." Then came the explosion. "We fell to the ground," Ola continued. "My leg was bleeding ... I tied the wound with the table cloth, calling out to him: 'Naseem, please, tell me you're okay ... please don't leave me.'" But he lay motionless on his back, bleeding heavily. "He was gone from the first moment."

Among those killed in the strike was Naseem Abu Sabha, whose fiancée, Ola, was wounded and hospitalised. The Israeli army and Shin Bet declared, without evidence, that Naseem was a "terrorist".

Naseem was taken by ambulance to the hospital before Ola. When she arrived there hours later for treatment, limping from the pain in her foot, her family was already there. Her father couldn't bear to look at her and didn't answer her anguished questions about whether or not Naseem had survived.

After she underwent a procedure to treat the torn tendons in her foot and she was released from the room in a wheelchair, the moment finally came. "He was martyred, right?" Ola asked her cousin. "He's in heaven now," came the reply.

They brought [his body] so I could say goodbye," Ola added. "He looked like a full moon — more beautiful than ever. I will miss him so much."

This article was updated on July 8, 2025 to incorporate the Israeli army and Shin Bet's statement from July 7 claiming that the strike on Al-Baqa had killed three militants, and to add Ola Abu Sabha's response to the allegation that her fiancée was one of them.

•

https://www.972mag.com/gaza-al-baqa-cafe-bombed-journalists/

"We live in a state of chaos"

10 July 2025
SOURCE: THE ELECTRONIC INTIFADA

> **Due to the mass displacements caused by the expansion of evacuation areas, and the lack of space free from rubble on which to set up camps, people are living wherever they can find space to pitch a tent.**

The port of Gaza, west of Gaza City, was once a beautiful place. Many residents would flock to the port daily and nightly to look at the boats, gather with family or take a stroll. It was also a hub for fishermen and other trades.

This is why its recent transformation this past May into a displacement zone, where thousands have sought basic refuge, is a shock to see. Memories of a once pleasant spot are now being obscured by the current reality of fear, hunger and poverty.

Muhammad Hamouda, 45, from Beit Lahiya in northern Gaza, has set up a tent with his wife and seven children. "The Israeli occupation forces dispersed leaflets urging people to evacuate Beit Lahiya, and we were worried about where to go," he said on 18 June, explaining that they took refuge at the port because no residential buildings were available to stay in. "After evacuating all the areas one by one, the [area] became crowded and people were crowded together," Hamouda said.

The port is now full of tents, with no paths separating the tents, he said. There is limited drinking water available at the port, Hamouda said, and his family must rely on water provided by aid organisations.

Despite the dire conditions at the port, people were still arriving after evacuating from the north because they had nowhere else to go. Over 680,000 people in Gaza have been newly displaced since March 2025, according to the United Nations. "Less than 18 percent of Gaza remains outside of Israeli-militarised zones or displacement orders," the UN reports.

Due to the mass displacements caused by the expansion of evacuation areas, and the lack of space free from rubble on which to set up camps, people are living wherever they can find space to pitch a tent. This has meant setting up tents in locations previously considered uninhabitable, like the port.

... /

> Siniora al-Radhi, 60, from Beit Lahiya, was displaced to the port with her children and grandchildren, 14 people in total. They are staying inside a single tent.

Hamouda has been forced to evacuate various shelters and homes due to Israeli attacks, and he is afraid it will happen yet again. "Our greatest fear is being evacuated from the Gaza port to another location, because movement and displacement are difficult due to the lack of adequate or safe space for the displaced."

"I fled on foot three weeks ago"

At the port on 18 June, one could feel a sense of depression and hopelessness among those displaced here. Every day, those living in tents wait for news of a ceasefire so they can simply access adequate amounts of food to feed their children.

Women at the port are facing the most strenuous conditions. Siniora al-Radhi, 60, from Beit Lahiya, was displaced to the port with her children and grandchildren, 14 people in total. They are staying inside a single tent. "I fled on foot three weeks ago, not knowing where I could go," she said. "I followed the people and walked with them until I found myself at the Gaza port."

She described the port as "not suitable" for living. "We used to come here before the war to improve our well-being, to see the fishermen and the sea, but the war has deprived us of everything," she said.

Her husband and several other family members were killed during Israeli strikes in Beit Lahiya. Several of her daughters have also lost their husbands and are now widows.

Despite all the loss and suffering, she said that, "the most difficult feeling we experience is hunger … Our children are starving, asking for bread and food. We only have lentils, and sometimes we don't find any, and we're forced to go to bed hungry," she said.

She said that the port now resembles Beit Lahiya, "because all the displaced people here are from Beit Lahiya." She described her living situation as incredibly precarious. "We live in a state of chaos due to the lack of security and the constant bombing". When there are Israeli air strikes near the port, she said she feels helpless. She does not have anywhere to run or hide from the bombs. "A cloth tent won't protect us from the missiles."

Due to the mass displacements caused by the expansion of evacuation areas, and the lack of space free from rubble on which to set up camps, people are living wherever they can find space to pitch a tent.

"Most difficult conditions of our lives"

Muhammad Rajab al-Masry, 37, was also displaced from Beit Lahiya to the port. In May, his mother was killed when the Israeli army bombed their home without warning. He had to leave his mother under the rubble and flee to another house in his neighbourhood with his cousin. Al-Masry was injured during the initial bombing of his home, and when it came time to evacuate, he felt compelled to go south, where his wife and three children had already evacuated.

"I didn't want to leave my area, but the army began targeting homes in a random and terrifying manner," he said. "They bombed the house my cousin and I had been in as soon as I left it." He fled on foot to the port and found his wife and three children.

"I used to love the port," he said, "but I no longer leave my tent to see the sea. I feel very sad about this place. I wake up dozens of times during the night to check on my children, whether they are alive or not." He described these days as "the most difficult conditions of our lives."

"Is it reasonable that I am by the sea and don't like seeing it because I am uncomfortable? My mother was martyred, and then my brothers and I were separated because our mother is the reason we are together."

Everyone feels rootless and aware that they are likely to be displaced again at any moment. They have lost the places that meant the most to them in their lives. "My message to the world is to view Gaza from a humanitarian perspective and pressure Israel to allow food to enter for civilians," said Muhammad Hamouda.

•

https://electronicintifada.net/content/we-live-state-chaos/50789

"We are starving"

21 July 2025
SOURCE: +972 MAGAZINE *

> **Every morning we wake up thinking of only one thing: how to find something to eat. My thoughts go immediately to our sick mother … we have nothing to offer her.**

My body is breaking down. My mother is collapsing from exhaustion. My cousin cheats death every day for a morsel of aid. Gaza's children are dying in front of our eyes, and we are powerless to help them. I am so hungry.

I've never meant those words in the way I do now. They carry a kind of humiliation that I can't fully describe. Every moment, I find myself wishing: If only this were just a nightmare. If only I could wake up and it would all be over.

Since last May, after I was forced to flee my home and take shelter with relatives in Khan Yunis refugee camp, I've heard those same words uttered by countless people around me. Hunger here feels like an assault on our dignity, a cruel contradiction in a world that prides itself on progress and innovation.

Every morning, we wake up thinking only of one thing: how to find something to eat. My thoughts go immediately to our sick mother, who had spinal surgery two weeks ago and now needs nutrition to recover. We have nothing to offer her.

Then there's my little niece and nephew — Rital, 6, and Adam, 4 — who ask for bread all the time. And we adults try to withstand our own hunger just to save whatever scraps we can for the kids and the elderly.

Since Israel imposed a total blockade on Gaza in early March (which it eased only marginally in late May), we haven't tasted meat, eggs or fish. In fact, we've gone without nearly 80% of the food we used to eat. Our bodies are breaking down. We feel constantly weak, unfocused and off-balance. We grow irritable easily, but most of the time we just stay silent. Talking uses up too much energy.

We try to buy anything available from the markets, but the prices are becoming impossible. A kilo, or two pounds, of tomatoes now costs NIS 90 (over US$25). Cucumbers are NIS 70 a kilo (around US$20).

… /

*Subsequently republished in *Pearl and Irritations* 31 July 2025. Accessed 29 August 2025.

> Since Israel imposed a total blockade on Gaza in early March ... we've gone without nearly 80% of the food we used to eat. Our bodies are breaking down. We feel constantly weak, unfocused and off-balance.

A kilo of flour is NIS 150 (US$45). These numbers feel outrageous and cruel. We survive on only one meal a day: usually just bread, made using whatever flour we managed to find. If we're lucky, lunch may include some rice, but even that doesn't fill us up. We try to set aside a little food for my mother, maybe some vegetables, but it's never enough. Most days, she's too weak to stand, too drained to even perform her prayers.

We rarely leave the house anymore, afraid our legs might give out. It already happened to my sister: while searching on the streets for something, anything, to feed her children, she suddenly collapsed to the ground. Her body didn't even have the strength to stay upright.

We began to sense the depth of the hunger crisis when the baker Abu Hussein, known to everyone in the camp, began scaling down his operations. He used to bake for dozens of families a day, including ours, who no longer have cooking gas or electricity to bake for themselves. From morning until night, his wood-burning ovens kept running. But recently, he was forced to start working fewer and fewer days each week. My sister would come home and say, "Abu Hussein's is closed. Maybe he'll work tomorrow." Now, trying to get dough and flour has become its own kind of suffering.

Three generations of hunger

In the camp, I came to understand the true cruelty of this genocide: the suffocating overcrowding, the mass of refugees forced out of their homes, and the endless stories of hunger.

I'm currently staying at my aunt's house; she took us in after we were displaced and has sheltered us for the past two months. Like nearly every other building in the camp, her home was almost completely destroyed by Israel's attacks. My aunt's siblings worked around the clock to repair what they could, managing to make one room liveable. The house overflows with grandchildren, each undergoing their own struggle with hunger. My oldest cousin, Mahmoud, is father to four of them. He himself has lost nearly 40 kgs (around 90 pounds) over the past few months. The signs of malnutrition are visible everywhere on his pale face and emaciated body.

> One day, Mahmoud came back with nothing. His face was drained of colour, and he looked like he might collapse. He told me the Israeli army had opened fire without warning. "The blood of a young man beside me splattered on my clothes," he said. "For a moment, I thought I was the one who'd been shot. I froze — I was sure the bullet was in my body."

Every day before dawn, Mahmoud sets out to the American-run aid distribution centres, risking his life to try to bring home some food for his starving kids. Since I arrived to stay with them, he has told me the same harrowing stories day after day.

"Today I crawled on my hands and knees through a crowd of thousands," he said recently, showing me a bag with scraps of food that he'd managed to scavenge. "I had to collect whatever had fallen to the ground — lentils, rice, chickpeas, pasta, even salt. My bones ache from being stepped on, but I have to do it for my children. I can't bear the sound of their hunger."

One day, Mahmoud came back with nothing. His face was drained of colour, and he looked like he might collapse. He told me the Israeli army had opened fire without warning. "The blood of a young man beside me splattered on my clothes," he said. "For a moment, I thought I was the one who'd been shot. I froze — I was sure the bullet was in my body". The young man fell to the ground right in front of him, but Mahmoud couldn't stop to help. "I ran more than six kilometres without looking back. My children are hungry and waiting for me to bring back food," he said, his voice breaking, "but they won't be happy if I come home dead."

My other cousin, Khader, is 28. He has a two-year-old daughter, and his wife is pregnant. He's consumed with worry about their unborn child, who is due two months from now. His wife isn't eating properly, and every day he sits in silence, tormented by the same questions: Will this famine harm my wife? Will the child she gives birth to be healthy or sick? His two-year-old, Sham, cries all day from hunger. She begs for bread — anything beyond the tasteless, heavy staples of rice, lentils, and beans that have upset her stomach and made her sick multiple times.

One day, a friend of Khader's gave him a handful of grapes for her. It was a small miracle. Khader knelt down beside Sham and offered her the grapes, but she only stared at them, playing with them in her tiny hands and refusing to eat them. She didn't recognise them: not once in her two years of life in Gaza had she seen grapes before. It wasn't until her father put one in his mouth and smiled that she hesitantly copied him. She chewed. Then she laughed.

... /

> **For about a month now I've lost the ability to follow the news. My focus is slipping. My body is breaking down ... for the past two days, I've been unable to swallow due to severe throat inflammation — a consequence of relying on dukkah and spicy red peppers to try to quell my hunger.**

Bodies shutting down

I often stand at the door of the house, watching the children in the camp. They spend most of their time sitting on the ground, staring blankly at passers-by. When I ask one of them to buy me an internet card so I can work, or call my niece from the neighbour's house, they respond in low, tired voices. They tell me they're hungry. That they haven't had bread in days.

I'm only 30 years old, but I'm no longer the energetic woman I once was. I used to work long hours between teaching and journalism, but since this war started I haven't had a moment's rest. I juggle exhausting household duties — caring for my mother and family — while simultaneously trying to keep documenting and writing about everything that's happening around me.

For about a month now, though, I've lost the ability to follow the news. My focus is slipping. My body is breaking down. I suffer from anaemia as a result of eating only lentils and other legumes for months. And for the past two days, I've been unable to swallow due to severe throat inflammation — a consequence of relying on dukkah and spicy red peppers to try to quell my hunger.

Mahmoud, a 28-year-old photographer who works with me on video stories, is struggling too. "I haven't eaten anything in two days except soup," he told me recently. "I don't have the energy to work." No one does. Working during a genocide requires a level of strength that is impossible to sustain. Starvation has crippled the productivity of every working person in Gaza.

Yesterday, I accompanied my mother to Nasser Hospital for a physical therapy session after her surgery. On the way we saw dozens of people who couldn't walk more than a few metres without having to rest. My mother was the same: her legs were too weak to carry her. She sat on a plastic chair by the roadside, gathering what little energy she could muster to go on.

As we continued walking, we heard shouting. Young men and women ran past, crying out in jubilation: "There are flour trucks on the street!" A huge crowd had formed. People were desperately sprinting toward the trucks for a chance at a bag of flour. It was chaos. No one was escorting the trucks to ensure that everyone

> "Tell me how to save my daughter Rahaf from death," she cried. "For a week she's eaten nothing but a single spoon of lentils each day ... They've taken away her right to live. I see death in her eyes."

could get their share safely. Instead, we watched the crowd race toward dangerous areas under the control of the Israeli army, just for flour. Some people made it back with bags. Others were killed. We saw bodies being carried away on men's shoulders, shot dead in the very places where aid was meant to save them.

18 deaths in 24 hours

After the therapy session, we left the hospital and passed women crying over their starving children, dying right before our eyes. One woman, Amina Badir, was screaming, clutching her three-year-old child. "Tell me how to save my daughter Rahaf from death," she cried. "For a week she's eaten nothing but a single spoon of lentils each day. She's suffering from malnutrition. There's no treatment, no milk at the hospital. They've taken away her right to live. I see death in her eyes."

According to the Health Ministry in Gaza, the death toll from hunger and malnutrition since 7 October 2023, has risen to 86 people, 76 of them children. On 20 July, it reported that 18 people had died of starvation in the previous 24 hours alone. Medical personnel staged a stand-in at Nasser Hospital to appeal for international intervention before more people starve to death.

I couldn't find a taxi to get us home. My mother waited at the hospital gate while I searched for transport, but fuel is scarce and taxis are virtually non-existent. I spent a full hour trying.

By the time I returned, I was dizzy and weak. I collapsed. I tried to stay strong for my mother, but there was no one else with us. Around me, I saw people fainting everywhere. One man said to me, "If there were proper food, your mother wouldn't have become this sick." We're all just trying to comfort one another in this endless famine. On Facebook, people pour out their anger, writing post after post about the Israeli starvation policy that has brought Gaza to its knees. We can no longer do the most basic things that people around the world do every day. Hunger has stripped us of everything.

•

https://www.972mag.com/hunger-gaza-food-aid-siege-children/

Ruwaida Amer with a group of her students before the current invasion. (Image courtesy of Ruwaida.)

Acknowledgments

Writing these stories was never easy. It took a lot of my energy, heart and soul, but they were all worth it so that the world knows the truth about what the people of Gaza are going through since the beginning of the war, and it is still not over. I am very grateful to my family who have supported me to continue my work. My mother has been very afraid for me moving around, but she is happy with my work. My father has spent long hours every day charging my devices to continue my work and has been happy knowing that my work was being read by the world. My sisters are also proud of my work, which has motivated me to continue. The support of my colleagues has also had a positive impact on my continuity.
I thank myself for my steadfastness and strength. The war changed my personality a lot, my way of thinking and my outlook on life. Despite all the sadness in my heart, I have become strong, patient and defiant of all difficulties and circumstances. I hope my message has been received and that you love Gaza as it loves the world and asks for peace and security.

— **Ruwaida Amer**

•

The editors are grateful to the following news outlets: +972 Magazine, abc News, Al Jazeera, The Electronic Intifada, Middle East Eye and Slate Magazine, where these stories were originally published, for allowing us to present them in this form.

The quotation from Mahmoud Darwish on page 2 is taken from a speech by the poet published in *Birzeit University: The Story of a National Institution*, edited by Ida Audeh. Birzeit University Publications, Birzeit, Palestine, 2010, p. 128.

The editors' work and Ian Robertson's design and typesetting for *Stories from the war on Gaza* have been undertaken pro bono. Additional thanks to Prue Marks of Ography for her generous assistance with the bookmarks and hyperlinks, also pro bono.

— **Paul Komesaroff, Sally Gardner**

•

www.ingramcontent.com/pod-product-compliance
Lightning Source LLC
Chambersburg PA
CBHW051158290426
44109CB00022B/2499